Over the Wall
More Escapes from 1

by
Trevor James

ORCHARD PUBLICATIONS
2 Orchard Close, Chudleigh, Devon TQ13 0LR
Telephone: (01626) 852714

ISBN 1 898964 71 8

Printed by
Hedgerow Print, Crediton, Devon EX17 1ES

ACKNOWLEDGEMENTS

I wish to thank Mr. John Lawrence, former Governor of Dartmoor Prison, for his generous help when preparing material for this book.

I owe much to the many friends and former colleagues at H.M.P. Dartmoor, past and present, for their recollections and unfailing patience in answering questions. In particular Prison Officer Mike Chamberlain who was more than generous and Mr. Brett Johnson, former Curator at Dartmoor Prison Heritage Centre. The present Curators, Mr. Dave Francis and Mrs. Laura Worth have also given liberal support. Officers of Devon and Cornwall Constabulary, serving and retired, who have been very supportive include Superintendent D.Roper (Rtd.), Sergeant K.Northey (Rtd.) and especially Police Constable Simon Dell, M.B.E.; Q.C.B., a firm friend and kindly critic who has contributed much.

I am grateful too for the kind assistance given by Mr. B.Estill (former Curator Devon and Cornwall Constabulary Museum); Mr. M.Ware (National Motor Museum, Beaulieu, Hants.); Mr. D.German (formerly of Princetown); and the late Mr. C.Waycott (Princetown resident) for information and pictures.

Pictures as acknowledged, others from author's collection.

CONTENTS.

AUTHOR'S PREFACE

The first *convict* prisoners arrived at Dartmoor on 2nd November 1850. On the 10th December 1850 the first escape occurred when three men absconded and it's been going on ever since. An escape-proof prison has not yet been built and probably never will be. The design and remote locations of the most secure jails in the world have failed to match the ingenuity of their inmates, who have overcome seemingly impossible obstacles and escaped. The most notorious of them, the island prison of Alcatraz in America, and the French penal establishment in the jungles of South America which included the infamous 'Devil's Island' (both are now defunct), failed to confine their prisoners with 100% effectiveness.

The history of Dartmoor Prison has a liberal sprinkling of escape stories, some of them more exciting than any work of fiction and so daringly executed even the authorities had a grudging admiration for the boldness and bravery of the prisoners involved in them. Sadly, many men have sought, and found, the most certain method of escape - suicide. Others have involuntarily 'escaped' into insanity. The public, who generally view escapees with alarm, have in the past often extended sympathy to them when they were caught, congregating to witness their return to custody amid cheering and shouts of encouragement as if they were heroes. It cannot be denied a romantic aura surrounds the spectacle of a man on the run (Great Train Robber Ronnie Biggs was a classic example) and a 'sporting' atmosphere has often been apparent on the moor when the latest sighting of a runaway or news of a housebreak, when clothes have been stolen and kitchens raided for food, were discussed in Dartmoor pubs with a light-heartedness certainly not shared by the victims.

Members of the public are often confused about the meaning of the various categories of prisoners. There are four categories: A, B, C, and D, each of which is directly related to an individual's escape potential.

Category A. Those who have the support and the means (possibly on the outside) for escape, or represent a threat to the public. These prisoners are confined in 'high security' prisons.

B Are a high escape risk but do not have the means.

C Are not a high escape or security risk, but may be 'opportunists'.

D Represent no risk whatsoever either of escaping or being a threat to the public.

The last two categories of prisoners are confined in Dartmoor Prison today.

Apart from the gangster types held at Dartmoor in the past, whose motives for escape were far from sentimental, most escapees have a domestic problem – jealousy or concern about a wife or girl friend for example. In the past a prisoner could clear his debts to other inmates by escaping or attempting to escape. An example of this happened some years ago at Channings Wood Prison near Newton Abbot, when an inmate successfully absconded and when he was clear of the prison calmly waited by the roadside for a lift back! A prison officer on his way to work kindly obliged. Then there are the 'opportunists' who see a chance to escape and take it there and then. Once they're out though they are often at a loss as to what to do. One man who ran away from the prison farm in 1995 was recognised and apprehended by an off-duty officer in Tavistock who saw him aimlessly walking the streets looking in shop windows.

What happens to recaptured prisoners? When Dartmoor was a War Prison (1809 - 1815) French and American escapees were locked up for ten days in the 'Black Hole', a twenty foot square dungeon without heating or bedding and on two thirds of their normal rations. If the military guards aided their escape those concerned faced a Court Martial and were sometimes shot; a flogging was the mildest punishment they could expect. A civilian helping an escapee got a public whipping, a term in the pillory, or transportation to the Colonies. Apprehending a prisoner who escaped brought a £5 reward and this practice continued well into the 20th century.

In the Victorian convict era a recaptured prisoner was punished by being placed in heavy chains and/or on a restricted diet (in multiples of three days bread and water interspersed by three days normal diet). The warders involved were charged with neglect of duty which resulted in a fine, reduction in rank, or loss of seniority. Until recently escapees were placed in solitary confinement until they were interviewed by the Governor who could award them up to forty two days loss of remission. They then spent six months on what was called the 'E' list which entailed strict precautions being taken to prevent them escaping again. Today they are transferred at once to a Category 'B' prison – most likely Exeter and placed on the 'E' list. Their presence is checked at intervals day and night and they are escorted everywhere they go inside the prison. They wear distinctive blue and yellow clothing and are allocated specially selected cells (these are positioned where the adjoining cells are always occupied, above and below and on each side). At night their clothes and eating utensils are taken from them, leaving them just their night attire. The 'E' list is reviewed every month. Loss of remission for escaping or attempting to escape is decided upon by an Independent Judiciary, usually a Judge.

On the whole escaping from prison is a very unattractive business but it's always going to happen and each incident brings its individual element of drama and excitement. Of the scores of prisoners who have gone 'over the wall' since Dartmoor accepted its first prisoner in 1809 some have been killed in the attempt; most of them were recaptured; all of them found the wide and lonely moor their most formidable guardian.

DARTMOOR PRISON

The prison was built during the war with Napoleon (1803—1814) to accommodate French prisoners of war previously held aboard the hulks (redundant men o' war converted for use as floating prisons) anchored off Plymouth. They were badly overcrowded and the death rate was unacceptably high which is why, with the number of prisoners taken continuing to rise, extra war prisons were required and Prince's Town as it was first called was one of the approved sites. Sir Thomas Tyrwhitt, who founded Princetown, laid the Foundation Stone in 1806 and the prison opened on 24th May 1809.

Two circular boundary walls nearly a mile in circumference enclosed five prison blocks, a hospital and a separate prison for the officers. Each block had three floors, two of which were of concrete and provided with rows of iron posts for the slinging of hammocks — no hardship involved here as most of the captives at this time were sailors. The top floors were wooden and intended for exercise in bad weather, but as the prison filled to capacity and became congested they too developed into dormitories and 1500 men were crammed into buildings designed to hold just 1,000. There were no windows, only a series of two foot square apertures

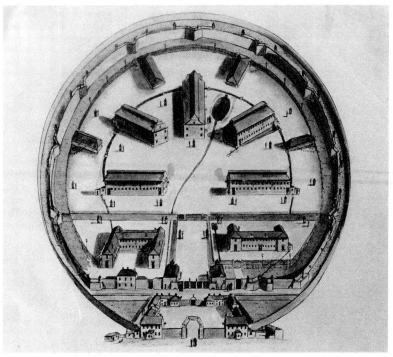

Dartmoor Prison, 1810. (From a painting by Paul Deacon).

3

for ventilation and no heating; the body heat of the mass of closely-packed men kept them alive in the depth of winter but the fetid atmosphere it created was the cause of disease, typhoid for example and chest complaints. By the year 1813, as a result of British military successes in the Peninsula campaign, Dartmoor was severely overcrowded. There were now more than 10,000 prisoners in a prison originally intended for 5,000 despite the fact two extra blocks were constructed in 1811. When American prisoners began arriving in 1813, mostly sailors captured during the War of 1812, the overcrowding got worse.

Their recreation was gambling and manufacturing model ships, trinkets, and various knick-knacks for barter at the market which was held each day within the prison where local traders sold poultry, vegetables, tobacco, coffee, and other commodities. The officer prisoners were those who either refused to live on parole or broke the parole rules. They engaged in theatricals, music, and art, funded by money sent to them by their families in France and lived the life of gentlemen by comparison with the men. The Americans were entirely different from the Frenchmen, being unruly and defiant, although a number of them like the French volunteered for paid work (slave labour was forbidden) building Princetown Church and the Parsonage.

About 1,250 Frenchmen died at Dartmoor Prison, nearly 500 of them during the first year (victims of a particularly virulent measles epidemic), the rest from typhoid and other diseases, as well as some who committed suicide and some who were killed in duels, or got shot trying to escape. The Americans suffered 271 known fatalities, most of them dying when there was an outbreak of smallpox in 1814. All the dead were buried in shallow pits outside the prison walls in the area which used to be part of the prison farm which closed in 2005. In 1865, by which time Dartmoor had been converted to a convict prison, the ground was scattered with bones which had surfaced due to erosion and the activities of animals. They were collected and divided by order of the Governor and interred in two mass graves surmounted by obelisks each of which was inscribed with the words: *Dulce et Decorum est pro Patria Mori* (it is Sweet and Honourable to Die for One's Country). The graves are situated in two separate areas at the rear of the prison.

When the wars ended the prisoners and their Military guards went home, leaving the prison in the hands of caretakers for the next thirty four years. For a short time it was leased to the British Naphtha Company who worked the peat bogs and constructed a tramway to transport the peat to the prison where retort furnaces had been installed for extracting the gas and oils (the track can still be traced over the moor below Fice's Well). Meanwhile the transportation of criminals was ending and another way of dealing with them had to be found. The solution was to establish Penal institutions where convicted men would work on projects similar to those performed in the Colonies and Dartmoor was one of the locations chosen.

French Prisoners of War in Dartmoor Prison. (From an oil painting by an unknown inmate).

In September 1850 one of the old prison blocks was converted for the confinement of convicts, which required the provision of separate cells. The concrete floors were removed in order to construct iron cells, arranged back to back with landings between them and the outside walls for the warders to patrol. The first inmates lived in perpetual gloom with candles for lighting after dark, the fit ones among them being put to work farming and quarrying. There was no recreation for them or the warders and the Silent Rule (no talking, whispering, or communication of any kind) was rigorously enforced. The convicts working outside the prison were guarded by units of the British Army at first, to be superseded later by the Civil Guard, a body of armed men comprised mainly of old soldiers. Prisoners laboured 'under the gun' for the next 100 years, during which time several were killed or maimed when guards opened fire on runaways. There was never a treadwheel at Dartmoor, nor were executions carried out there, but in common with other establishments punishments were severe: flogging with the 'cat o' nine tails' or the birch for serious offences; restricted diet (as explained in the preface), the wearing of heavy chains, canvas suits and being placed in solitary confinement, are examples of how discipline was kept. Flogging, restricted diet, and armed guards for outside work parties were the norm until the 1950s and beyond.

The prison has changed dramatically since those early times. Four of the original blocks were demolished in the late 1800s and new granite buildings took their place. They have held some of the worst rogues and criminals this country has ever known. Among them were the 'Titchbourne Claimant', whose fraudulent claim to a missing (presumed drowned in a shipwreck) aristocrat's inheritance resulted in the longest trial in British legal history; John George Haigh, dubbed 'the acid bath murderer' for killing a widow, after charming her into parting with her money and disposing of the body by dissolving it in a bath of sulphuric acid (he served time at Dartmoor for fraud before committing the murders for which he was found guilty and hanged) and James Camb, a former ship's steward who was convicted of murdering the actress Gay Gibson on board the Union Castle liner 'Durban Castle' and dumping her body in the sea (it was the first murder conviction without a body being produced and he was probably the first man to be sentenced to death then reprieved when hanging was abolished). Then there was the 'Mad Axeman' Frank Mitchell whose story is the first to be told in this book. The Irish have featured in Dartmoor's past too, starting with members of the Fenian organisation from the 1860s onwards. Mr. Eamon De Valera, who became Prime Minister and President of the Republic of Ireland was jailed for taking part in the Easter rising in Dublin in 1916 and served part of his sentence on the 'moor'. In 1939 a number of I.R.A. members were in custody following a bomb incident in Coventry.

In 1917 convicts were transferred elsewhere and the prison was turned into a Work Centre for more than 1,000 'Conscientious Objectors' who chose to go to prison rather than abandon their (mostly religious) principles by going to the war.

Dartmoor Prison has been extensively modernised in recent years and inmates now have electric lighting, central heating and telephone contact with their families, a far cry from the days when a man practically lost all contact with the outside world for the duration of his sentence. Prisoners are treated more humanely now than ever before and the harsh conditions that gave Dartmoor its fearsome reputation no longer apply. In common with other establishments it has updated its facilities and plays its part in new initiatives aimed at helping offenders. There are some who say a prison sentence is 'easy', but to be deprived of liberty can be a devastating experience. A Dartmoor inmate lives and eats alone in his cell and the hours he spends working or training, taking exercise, and the two hours a day allocated for Association, are the only occasions when he has contact with his fellow men. When the key turns to lock him in his cell at 8.00 p.m. he finds himself alone with his thoughts and his conscience, just like the convicts of old.

New arrivals to Dartmoor Prison, early 20th century. (Courtesy Dartmoor Prison Heritage Centre).

FRANK MITCHELL - THE 'MAD AXEMAN'

There was never an escape from prison that caught the public's attention more than that of Frank Mitchell who disappeared from an outside work party in December 1966. It was a typical winter day on Dartmoor, windy, cold and wet, when 'Big Frank' literally vanished. Stories about his eventual fate vary, but there can be no doubt he was assisted by London based criminals and was later murdered.

Dartmoor Prison officers remember him as a man who rejoiced in his enormous physical strength and took every opportunity to show it off. A gentle giant with the mind of a child, he would instantly turn into a raging bull of a man if something upset him; yet in the main he was a trouble free inmate providing he was constantly humoured and tactfully handled. For a big man he wasn't tall, under six foot with very broad shoulders and a huge chest; 'stocky' would be an appropriate word to use in describing him. The newspapers dubbed him 'The Mad Axeman' but Frank wasn't 'mad' in the true sense of the word and neither was he a murderer. He was certainly a tough and highly dangerous individual who 'ruled the roost' unopposed over his fellow inmates. He arrived at Dartmoor with a fearsome reputation, not solely on account of the physical violence he was capable of but also because, during a previous term of imprisonment, he was suspected of slashing another inmate with a 'chiv' (a home made knife). When he was allowed to join outside work parties, against the advice of experienced officers, several people living on or near the moor openly expressed fears for their safety. The late James Mildren, a well known and respected local journalist, was approached on at least two occasions by a lady who lived on the edge of the moor who was frightened and wanted reassurance. He raised the matter with the prison, but to no effect; yet when Mitchell went missing there was a national outcry and the Home Secretary faced a barrage of criticism over the decision to permit such a man to work outside the prison. To understand this we need to examine Mitchell's record. He was born in Kennington in the Borough of Lambeth in 1929, and attended a special school for backward children. He became a delinquent at an early age and graduated to crime where his activities included housebreaking, office breaking and ultimately robbery with violence, all of which earned him terms of imprisonment. He was friendly with the three Kray brothers and corresponded with them when he was in prison (he helped out now and then on 'The Firm' as they called themselves). He was an unruly, violent inmate and in two recorded instances corporal punishment was administered.

Pentonville 1954.   15 strokes with the 'cat o' nine tails' for gross personal violence. He had assaulted three warders.

Hull Prison 1962.   15 strokes with the birch for attacking two warders.

In 1955 he was sent to Rampton Mental Hospital after being certified mentally defective and later to Broadmoor. He escaped from both institutions and whilst on the run from Broadmoor robbed an elderly couple in their home after threatening them with an axe, thus earning his title 'The Mad Axeman'. In 1958 at Berkshire Assizes he was found not to be certifiable and sentenced to ten years plus life imprisonment for robbery with violence with no fixed date for his release.

When he was transferred to Dartmoor in September 1962 the then Chief Director of Prisons stipulated he was not to be employed outside the prison without reference to the Commissioners of Prisons. Mitchell was classed as a trouble-maker and potential escaper which meant he was immediately placed on the 'Escape List'. He seemed to settle down however because within a year he was off the 'E' List and in May 1964 joined the quarry party although this was against the advice of experienced officers. He eventually became a familiar sight in Princetown when he graduated to other outside work parties.

At Dartmoor stories about Frank Mitchell are numerous and impressive. One retired prison officer who knew him well said: "He was a giant of a man, a fitness fanatic who was always exercising in his cell or at work. He would pick up iron bars, boulders, in fact anything to hand and lift them above his head. On one occasion an inmate, a heavily-built man, was injured in the quarry and I was about to send for a stretcher when Mitchell intervened. 'No need for that, Guv,' he said, 'I'll carry him for you'. 'You will never do it' I told him - but he did. I helped get the casualty on his shoulders and he carried him non-stop all the way to the prison and into the hospital, a distance of half a mile or more". Another officer recalls how Mitchell once lifted two officers at once in a 'bear hug', one under each arm. 'It was his idea of being playful, but his regular minders kept out of his way because he'd broken an officer's bones doing that in another prison – he didn't know his own strength'. Yet another ex-prison employee tells how he got hold of the prison Governor, Mr. Denis Malone and lifted him in the air. 'Come on Frank, put me down there's a good chap' he said and he was set down unharmed. Tales about Frank carrying a 3 cwt. sack of coire from the stores to the mat making shop, and lifting the rear of a Triumph Vitesse police car on the forecourt of what is now the High Moorland Visitor Centre with two officers inside and turning it 180 degrees, are enshrined in Dartmoor's history. It appears the only way to manage Mitchell was to humour him, and this helps explain why he was allowed a degree of freedom and tolerance not permitted to other inmates. He sort of tagged along on the work parties with no intention of working, carrying an axe on his ample shoulders, thus perpetuating the 'Axeman' title he bore. Mr. Malone, who was a very fair-minded Governor, considered it was wrong for him to be detained indefinitely and tried to get him a release date from the Home Secretary. Whether or not Mitchell knew about this is uncertain, but it turned out it was his prime motive for escaping and he (Mitchell) sought to bring it to the attention of the public and the Home Secretary in letters he wrote to two national newspapers whilst in hiding after his escape. Ironically, the Home Secretary, under questioning in the Commons, stated Mitchell's case was already under review with the intention of fixing a date for his release. It was too late – the bird had flown.

One Sunday in December 1966 a large Rover car was seen in the Two Bridges area by the Vicar of Princetown, the late Reverend Courtney Johns and his wife. On a winter day in the 1960s such a sight was rare, and the Vicar decided to report what he'd seen to the police. The same car had called at the Forest Inn at Hexworthy, not far from Princetown and three very well dressed men with London accents had lunch there. They were visiting an acquaintance at Dartmoor Prison they told the landlord. Was that acquaintance Frank Mitchell and was the purpose of their visit to formulate an escape plan? It seems more than likely because just a couple of weeks later their car was again spotted on the moor the day before the 'Big Escape' took place.

Police Constable Roper, the resident Princetown policeman, making an enquiry during the hunt for Mitchell.

Mitchell's work party were engaged in repairing fences at Bagga Tor, about eight miles from the prison. They were taken there each morning by minibus and collected in the afternoon to be returned to the prison. Lunch was taken in a hut close by, and prepared by one of the prisoners from supplies they brought with them. Men who were selected for the 'Honour Parties' as they were called then, were those with only a short time left to serve and who had good behaviour records (all the more remarkable Mitchell was included). Just one officer was in charge and because some prisoners necessarily worked beyond his field of vision (they were strung out over a two mile long fence), it would have been easy for any one of them to slip away unobserved. Mitchell, it seems, was in the habit of doing just that, and when the story of his escape appeared in the newspapers together with his photograph, there were several local people, including some landlords, who recognised him as a regular visitor to their village pubs. On one occasion he took a taxi to Tavistock and bought a budgerigar. Statements confirming these events were made on oath at the subsequent trial of the three Kray brothers and some of their associates, on charges of aiding Mitchell to escape, harbouring him, and murdering him. An astonished Judge Lawton declared: 'It all sounds cloud cuckoo to me!', a sentiment he shared with an equally astonished British public.

On the afternoon of Monday 12th December 1966 the weather was atrocious on Dartmoor and Mitchell's party took shelter in their hut. Frank left the hut on the pretext of going to feed some ponies and did not reappear. There was no radio communication with the prison in those days and when he failed to turn up for the journey back the officer in charge raised the alarm by telephoning from a public call box in Peter Tavy, the nearest village. Princetown's resident policeman, Constable D. Roper, was at Postbridge on an enquiry when the prison rang to say Frank Mitchell was reported missing from a work party. It was his wife Rosemary who took the call. 'I was frightened and locked all the doors and windows,' she told the author, 'it was the only time during our posting to Princetown I was ever scared, but I was alone in the house with darkness coming on and two young children to care for. I was quite apprehensive'. Mrs. Roper, like all Princetown residents, knew that escaped prisoners always headed away from the town, but who could say what a 'Mad Axeman' might do? She was not the only person to be alarmed by Mitchell's escape. A man living with his wife in Mount Tavy Road on the outskirts of Tavistock later confessed to keeping a gun under his bed after hearing the news.

One of the biggest manhunts ever mounted for an escaped Dartmoor prisoner was then organised. The police set up road blocks and officers with tracker dogs searched moorland farms, outhouses, cattle sheds and barns. They were assisted in scouring the moors and commons by soldiers of the Wessex Brigade, Royal Marine Commandos from 41 Commando, Bickleigh, and men of the Argyll and Sutherland

Highlanders from Seaton Barracks, Crownhill (now closed). Prison officers were allocated to search parties looking for the man the Press called 'the most dangerous criminal in England' and a Royal Air Force helicopter from Chivenor, north Devon, was called in to help. They were still looking for Mitchell at Christmas. On 29th December a retired prison officer who had known him when he was serving at Broadmoor made a personal appeal to him on nation-wide television to give himself up. 'Frank', he said, 'you've made your point, and the sooner you give yourself up the better your case will be... if you wish to approach me I will do all I can to assist you and convey you to the authorities'. He went on to say he thought Mitchell could be trusted in certain circumstances but he objected to uniformed authority — it was a 'red rag' to him. It was a wasted effort because by then Frank Mitchell was dead, murdered by persons unknown; in any case we now know he was off the moor and on the road to London before he was reported missing.

On Sunday 11th December, the day before the escape, the big Rover car turned up again at the Forest Inn at Hexworthy and three muscular, smartly dressed men had breakfast. In the afternoon two of them were admitted as visitors to Dartmoor Prison, using what were later found to be false names. That evening a garage attendant in Tavistock spoke to them on the forecourt when they asked for a map of the area; when they were told there was not one available they drove off after receiving directions on how to get to Peter Tavy, a village near Bagga Tor where Mitchell's party was working. It seems certain they picked up Frank Mitchell by arrangement the next day and by nightfall he was installed in a flat in East Ham, London. When prison clothing with his prison number stamped on it was found a day or two later in a lay-by at Tedburn St. Mary, between Okehampton and Exeter on the old main A 30 road leading out of the county, the search was extended to the London area. Armed police visited the homes of known criminals who might have been harbouring him, but without success.

'Big Albert' Donaghue, a member of the Kray gang, confessed years later to being involved in Mitchell's escape. 'We was waiting in the car outside the phone box at Peter Tavy when Frank came running round the corner, large as life' he said. He went on to say they drove directly to a council flat in London rented by another associate called Dunn where Mitchell was to live for another eleven days.

Meanwhile an embarrassed Home Secretary and a new Dartmoor Prison Governor (Mr. Malone had retired to New Zealand) were having to explain several anomalies concerning one of the most sensational episodes in the entire history of the prison. What was a man like Mitchell doing in Dartmoor in the first place? Shouldn't he have been sent back to Broadmoor or a similar institution? Why was he permitted to join an outside work party with a history of violence, previous escapes and an indefinite period still to serve? Why was the advice of senior prison officers not to

12

allow Mitchell outside the prison ignored? These are some of the questions which were asked in the House of Commons by Mr. Michael Heseltine, M.P. for Tavistock. As a result a Committee of Enquiry, which had been set up under Lord Louis Mountbatten to enquire into the circumstances surrounding the escape of the convicted spy, George Blake, from Wormwood Scrubs in October 1966, was given the additional task of investigating recent events at Dartmoor. A high security fence, floodlighting, the formation of a prison dog section, and (to the prison officer's delight) a radio communication system were among the enquiry's recommendations, all of which were implemented.

'Big Frank' was killed on 23rd December after only eleven days of 'freedom' cooped up in the London flat; no-one was convicted of his murder and his body was never found. Ronald Kray, in his book *My Story* (Pan Books) claims he knows who killed Mitchell and names an associate, Billy Exley, who, he says, was paid to take him out of the country with the help of three Greeks and that they murdered him instead. It was Exley who later tipped off the police it was the Krays who did it and gave evidence for the prosecution at their trial. Whoever was responsible what did the murderers do with the body? The story is told within the Prison Service that several prisoners, whilst being transferred from one prison to another, have pointed out to their escorts the same concrete pillar supporting a motorway bridge which, they say, is where Mitchell's corpse was disposed of in a mix of concrete. Another account alleges his killers studied the funeral notices in the newspapers and put his body in a ready dug grave late at night, under the lining. The legal occupant was afterwards interred on top and Frank Mitchell was lost to the world for ever.

In 1999 gang member Freddie Foreman, who had been acquitted on a charge of murdering Frank Mitchell and knew he couldn't be charged twice for the crime, appeared on a television programme *The Krays – Unfinished Business* where he admitted shooting him repeatedly together with a man called Alfie Gerard. The body was allegedly dumped overboard off Newhaven from a boat on a smuggling run to Belgium and France. (See *Nipper Read —The Man Who Nicked the Krays* by Detective Superintendent Leonard Read and James Morton, Little, Brown & Co. 2001).

It is for the reader to decide who to believe from the accounts given by professional rogues and criminals. Two Prison Chaplains who made assessments of Mitchell in prison have the last word. One of them strikes an optimistic note after finding him reading poetry in his cell: 'This man has a fund of fearlessness and courage which could, in other circumstances, have made him a very useful citizen'. The second is prophetic and nearer the truth one feels: 'A tough-seeming, but weak, impressionable, young man, fond of posing as the toughest of the boys....*there seems almost no hope for his future*'. (Author's italics).

13

THE INSPECTOR

A prisoner escaped from a work party outside Dartmoor Prison several years ago and later stole a car. Meanwhile police check points were set up and every road leading off the moor was quickly sealed. The check point at Moorshop between Tavistock and Princetown was particularly busy and there was a long 'tailback' of vehicles waiting to be checked when a Plymouth Police Inspector arrived on the scene. He found his men coping well, but having to deal with a number of impatient motorists and as sometimes happens, one or two tried to sneak past, pretending they were unaware they had to stop the same as everybody else. One car crawled by on the outside without stopping and incurred the extreme displeasure of the Inspector who ticked him off before sending him on his way with a proverbial 'flea in his ear'.

Later on, back at the station, a tired and irate Inspector tossed his cap onto his desk muttering about the impatient oaf in the blue Morris 1000 who didn't have the sense to realise everyone had to be checked and deliberately 'jumped' the queue. There was a ghastly silence... 'Did you say a blue Morris 1000, sir?' a voice said, 'the man we're looking for stole one at Princetown'. There was a flurry of activity as the details and direction the car was heading in were circulated. The vehicle was soon found, not far from where it was last seen, but there was no sign of the wanted man who had somehow eluded the police cordon and disappeared (he was eventually detected somewhere in France and returned to custody having earned a prominent place in Dartmoor's escape records).

Now that a respectable period of time has elapsed, the story can be told, but in Devon today there is a Senior Police Officer who would prefer to forget this incident ever happened.

A VERY DETERMINED YANKEE

The winter of 1813 – 1814 was the worst for more than fifty years on Dartmoor. The snow began falling in November interspersed with hail and rain and by the end of the month the ground was already white.

There were nearly 10,000 prisoners of war in the Prisoner of War Depot in Princetown at this time. Most of them were French with a sprinkling of men from those nations either allied with France or under occupation by Napoleon's armed forces. In addition there were several hundred American prisoners who were captured in the War of 1812 which still raged on the American and Canadian mainland and on the seas. With the American War of Independence still fresh in the minds of their captors, many of whom still regarded Americans as 'rebels', their treatment was far worse than was either necessary or proper. The French were well versed in prison ways and had established a set pattern of everyday life, manufacturing models, toys and knick-knacks for sale or barter at the daily market allowed within the Depot. In addition a number of them were earning a small wage (slave labour was forbidden by agreement on both sides) as builders (the Church of St. Michael and All Angels for example although this was afterwards completed by American prisoners) sweepers, barbers, nurses in the infirmary, and waiters to the Officers who were imprisoned with them. By contrast the 'Yankees', as they were known, were kept separate from the main body of prisoners and denied access to the market where they could have purchased tobacco, coffee, fresh vegetables, poultry, etc. Instead they traded their few pitiful belongings and even their shoes, blankets, clothing and ultimately their rations to unscrupulous Frenchmen all too eager to take advantage of them in return for a 'chew of baccy' or some soap or other comforts. One of the most trying burdens they had to bear was the early morning 'turnout' when they were paraded in the yards for a roll call that sometimes took hours to complete. Many of them were without shoes or stockings and some had cut up their blankets to cover their bodies and their feet, and although several men collapsed each day from the cold and had to be carried to the hospital in a state of hypothermia, the routine continued relentlessly. All protests were answered with the reply it was a requirement of the Transport Board who administered the custody of prisoners of war.

It was against this background that eight Americans determined to make their escape at any cost. In December 1813 the cold worsened to the extent nearly all the Yankees stayed in their hammocks which, being packed closely side by side and in tiers five high, ensured the men's body heat was transmitted from one to another and literally kept them alive in the stone dormitories they occupied without heating and only wooden shutters to keep out the draught through the unglazed 'windows'. Toward the end of the month it snowed every day and the cold was intense.

An old picture of Princetown's Church of St. Michael's and All Angels, built by French and American prisoners of war.

On New Years Day the temperature plummeted further and in just four hours buckets of water froze solid as did the running leat that supplied the drinking water. Everyone was compelled to eat snow to alleviate their thirst. The Yankees again kept to their beds for warmth whilst outside the snow was two foot thick and getting higher daily until the drifts within the prison reached almost to the top of the two boundary walls. The sentries who manned the walls were permitted to stand down, such was the severity of the cold, and they retired to their guardrooms which were situated in the area between the walls called the Military Walk. At midnight on the 14th January 1814 eight stalwart Americans decided to take advantage of this to make their escape, an indictment if ever there was one of the severity of the treatment which prompted them to take such a formidable risk.

With the aid of a makeshift ladder they easily got over the inner wall, taking advantage of the high snowdrifts and descended to the Military Walk where they prepared to scale the outside boundary wall to freedom. Sadly for them they had entered this area adjacent to one of the guardrooms and the soldier guards were alerted and apprehended seven of them. The eighth man got over the wall and disappeared into the frozen wastes of the moor.

The recaptured men were placed in the 'Cachot' which was a separate stone hut twenty foot square without heating and on two thirds rations. It was the normal punishment for attempting to escape but with the weather so severely cold it was a terrible thing to endure. Meanwhile their comrade had survived the frightful conditions on the moor for a day and a night, an outstanding feat of endurance. On his second day at large without food or shelter he stumbled on a remote cottage and was taken in by the inhabitants. They of course guessed at once who he might be and at the first opportunity returned him to the Depot where he joined his friends in the Cachot. He had been given up for dead by prisoners and guards alike and on his return the officers and soldier guards were so impressed by his fortitude and resilience they openly stated that if they had their way he would be set free. Whether or not their sentiments were noted we will never know but Captain Thomas Shortland R.N. the Agent in charge of the Depot and who had only just taken over from Captain M. Gambier R.N. took pity on them all and ordered them to be taken back to their respective prison blocks. One of their fellow prisoners composed the following lines in celebration of this unusual and gallant action:

On the 14th day of January
This night ordained by fate,
For eight poor Yankee sailors
To try for their escape.

Seven of these detected were,
And in the Guardhouse lay;
The eighth resolved on liberty
By chance he got away.

The night being dark and dreary,
And he had far to go,
So this poor Yankee sailor
Got hobbled in the snow.

Discovered by his enemies
That forced him back again,
Within the walls of Dartmoor
Oppressed with cold and pain.

Shortland, bred a seaman,
In Neptune's school; was taught
His heart compressed with pity
Methinks I read his thought –

Saying 'Go into the Guardhouse
And set those eight men free;
I'll show the sons of liberty
There's honour still in me'.

And so the eight men survived. Not only that but the morning roll call was abolished and a number of Americans were permitted to attend the market. Yet for all the sympathy and understanding they received from Captain Thomas Shortland his name was loathed by them just fifteen months later in the wake of the 'Princetown Massacre' when the American prisoners were fired upon by the guards – but that is another story.

The American Cemetery and Memorials at Dartmoor Prison.

GASKEN AGAIN

It was all over in a flash. Prisoners were repairing a roof at Dartmoor Prison when suddenly two of them made a dash for the boundary wall carrying the ladder they'd been using. The officers in charge (whose priority was to guard the remaining prisoners) watched helplessly as they scrambled to the top of the wall, pulled the ladder up and over it and disappeared down the other side.

This was a classic Dartmoor Prison escape on another cold winter day with a thick mist that gave the fugitives every advantage. It was Tuesday 16th November 1932 and the newly installed siren howled its first warning, summoning every available warder to join the hunt for the missing men. One of them, John Michael Gasken, aged 32 and serving five years penal servitude for housebreaking and forgery, had escaped from Dartmoor in February the previous year and was recaptured with the aid of bloodhounds in Plymouth. 'I didn't know what Dartmoor was like and I'll never try it again' he said having suffered from exposure and being admitted to the prison hospital with pneumonia; yet here he was fleeing over the moors once more, hunted like a wild animal by more than 100 warders and police, many of them armed. His companion was Frederick Amey, 44 years old and serving three years penal servitude for housebreaking and receiving stolen property. The exercise developed into one of the biggest manhunts in Dartmoor Prison's history and involved the first search by aeroplane for escaped convicts.

On hearing the alarm every available warder was soon speeding to his allotted post on the moor, some on horseback, others in cars, on motorcycles, bicycles and on foot in an attempt to seal off the area and contain the escapees. The weather was atrocious even by Dartmoor standards: there was a biting easterly wind, continuous heavy rain and a dense mist which made driving conditions extremely hazardous. Two *Western Morning News* reporters who followed the hunt by car wrote a graphic account of how slow and hazardous their progress was in the dense fog with one of them leaning out of the car window and directing the driver to 'bear right' or 'go left' as the case might be (there were no 'cats eyes' or white road markings then). There was no sign of the fugitives however – they disappeared into the mist and the rain soon erased any traces of footprints.

Michael Gasken and Frederick Amey.

In the days that followed reports of sightings, break-ins and other suspicious occurrences came from a number of localities over a wide area, not only on the moor but from the Plymouth, Gunnislake (East Cornwall) and Morwellham districts. All had to be investigated, stretching the search parties to the limit. One incident involved two men seen running on the moor near Hexworthy and resulted in a frantic dash to the area by warders and police with dogs*, but without result. Another incident triggered a search near Chagford which proved to be another false alarm.

*Neither the police nor the prison had a dog section at this time. Sometimes bloodhounds were borrowed from local residents – on this occasion from Miss Lowe of Shaugh Prior. The best of them was a blind dog named 'Smuggler'.

It was now late on Wednesday and some of the warders had been on duty for twenty four hours and had not slept for thirty six hours. They were relieved and recalled for food and rest, whilst in the prison all prisoners had to be kept locked up because of the resulting staff shortages. Out on the moor where the temperature was barely above freezing a warder commented to a reporter how the bitterly cold wind had penetrated their thick coats and God help the men on the run clad in just their prison clothing. The search continued on Thursday but there was still no sign of the two men, only further incidents that had to be investigated but proved to have no connection with the business in hand.

Then came a break-through. Early on Friday morning the first sound evidence of the prisoner's whereabouts occurred with the discovery of a break-in at the railway station in Horrabridge which was on the GWR Plymouth to Launceston line, a single track railway long since closed. Chocolate and cigarette machines were damaged and the contents taken as well as two overcoats and a cap. A significant find was the imprint of a nailed boot which was examined by the prison boot maker and positively identified as a convict footprint. Police with bloodhounds rushed to the scene and quickly took off after a strong scent but to their dismay the trail led through a field with a flock of sheep and all trace of it was lost.

On Saturday, with reports still coming in from different locations and the search teams nearing the end of their tether, Major L. Morris, M.C., the Chief Constable of Devon and former Dartmoor Prison Governor, decided on a new approach. He hired an aeroplane from Haldon Airfield near Exeter and flew as observer with the pilot Mr. W.R. Parkhouse to scour the Gunnislake and Gulworthy region. A huge area was covered in a short period and eliminated from the search. However there was a close shave for the escaped convicts when the aircraft later flew over Lydford Gorge between Tavistock and Okehampton where another reported sighting had led to search parties with soldiers being deployed. The pilot's attention was drawn to a white terrier dog fretting around some bushes but he and Major Morris concluded it had probably seen a rabbit. In fact Gasken and Amey were hiding there and desperately trying to shoo it away when Amey looked up and said to his companion 'I bet that's Major Morris in that bloody plane!' It was afterwards revealed the searchers on the ground were within yards of the two men but luck was still with them and they remained undetected.

Sunday brought fresh clues and the Chief Constable now recognised the truth of what he already suspected — Gasken and Amey were hiding by day and moving by night, mainly along the railway tracks. A house near Okehampton railway station called 'Partlands' belonging to a Mr. Robinson was broken into that day and food taken (bread, kippers, butter, apples and a saucepan to cook with). A railway worker's hut further up the line was later entered where they were able to enjoy their feast. The two men were now on the double-tracked Southern Railway main line from Plymouth to Waterloo which passed through Tavistock, Lydford, Okehampton and Exeter. The old GWR and Southern Railway lines converged and ran side by side between Tavistock and Lydford. Gasken and Amey must have

Major Morris, centre, and pilot W. R. Parkhouse discuss the hunt for the escaped convicts with PC 59 of the Devon Constabulary before taking off from Haldon Aerodrome. (Reproduced courtesy of Mr K. Saunders, author of 'Devon Aerodromes in old Photographs).'

realised which line could best be used in their favour. They were heading for Exeter believing (rightly) that if they could elude the police cordons there they had a good chance of avoiding capture. When a house near Crediton was raided for food (a quantity of jewellery was ignored) a piece of cloth was discovered and identified as prison material. It was afterwards learned Gasken had torn up his cap to bandage his feet. Major Morris decided now was the time to act upon his conviction and prepare a trap.

Two police teams were assembled the following day in readiness for a night operation. The County Police force supplied seventy officers to patrol after dark along the line of the railway in a 'V' formation from Crediton towards Exeter whilst Exeter City Police worked the main line towards them from Exeter St. Davids Station. Warders from Princetown were on stand-by at Crediton ready to move in any direction they might be required. It spelled the end of a determined run by the two convicts. At 9.20 pm they were spotted on the railway track and when challenged jumped over a hedge and ran for it hotly pursued by Sgt. Greet and P.C. Sangster of Exeter City Police. Both men offered little resistance and surrendered, tired and hungry after their ordeal. To the officer's surprise Amey and Gasken were clean shaven. They had a razor blade jammed in a cleft stick and with just water for lather had managed to avoid an unkept appearance; both of them wore the stolen overcoats from Horrabridge Station over their prison clothes to add to an outward show of respectability. After spending the night at Exeter Police headquarters they were collected by Dartmoor warders and returned by car to the prison where they were placed in the punishment cells to await sentencing for their misdemeanours.

The Prison Governor was Major Charles Pannell, O.B.E., M.C., D.S.O., a firm disciplinarian and very able administrator who had been specially chosen to take over at Dartmoor after the famous convict mutiny earlier that year. He visited both men in the punishment cells where Amey, who had fallen into a river whilst on the run and contracted pneumonia, asked permission to keep the extra blanket he had been given. When this was refused the Governor was assaulted and knocked to the ground. This earned the culprit an additional penalty in the form of a flogging with the dreaded cat o' nine tails.

One of the most gruelling escape episodes in the history of the moorland jail was brought to an end by the perseverance and commitment to duty of police and warders not to mention the inspired leadership and conviction of Chief Constable Morris.

YOUNG MISS HILL

One of the most remarkable features of the second Gasken escape was the assistance rendered to the authorities by twenty two year Miss Dorrie Hill whose father Mr. Herbert Hill was Foreman of Works at the prison. At a time when most ordinary people did not know how to drive, to see a woman behind the wheel was a rare event. Her father had taught her the basics and her driving 'test', supervised by him, was a trip down Countisbury Hill in north Devon, a notoriously steep road with dangerous bends. In his opinion if you could safely negotiate this you were capable of driving anywhere! Now her father's judgment was justified under the most difficult circumstances imaginable and earning the gratitude of prison warders who were being ferried to and from where they were needed. Picture

Miss Hill with her cargo of warders all anxious to get to the scene, driving night and day, tired like everyone else and responsible for the safety of her passengers in torrential rain and the worst of Dartmoor mists.

Governor Pannall would have had his hands full with official enquiries and investigations concerning the escape, but despite this he took the trouble to write a charming and sincere letter of thanks to Miss Hill for her assistance over a period of six miserable days. It read:

24th. November 32   *H.M. Prison*
                                                                                     Dartmoor

Dear Miss Hill

On behalf of the prison Officers I should like to thank you for your assistance during the recent escape. The use of your car greatly facilitated the movements of the officers both with speed and comfort. Furthermore driving at night on strange roads through mist and rain called for physical endurance and pluck which you have clearly shown is not the monopoly of the male side of the family.

Yours sincerely,

Pannall. Major.
Governor H.M. Prison Dartmoor.

(Photograph of Dorrie Hill and Major Pannall's letter reproduced courtesy Dartmoor Prison Heritage Centre).

KEYS

One day in March 1862 a Dartmoor warder on patrol saw a prisoner named Anderson look out from the doorway of his cell. The warder's astonishment could only have been matched by Anderson's dismay. After taking him away to be locked up again the warders carried out a search of his cell and found a skeleton key that had been painstakingly made by an unlucky escapee who happened to pick the wrong moment to look and see if the coast was clear. Six years previously, on 25th August 1856, it was a warder who was unlucky. Convict James Lake had made a duplicate cell key out of bone salvaged from his meat ration. He fitted it to a piece of stick, put his arm through the ventilation slot adjacent to the door of his iron cell, and managed to insert it into the lock outside. After getting out of his cell he used the key again to liberate another man and together they overpowered the night warder, but their escape attempt was foiled when, during the struggle, the warder's cries alerted his colleagues who were quickly on the scene to apprehend the two convicts and lock them up once more.

Prisoners have been making duplicate keys ever since the convict prison opened and Dartmoor Prison's Heritage Centre has a collection of them, most of which were confiscated during routine cell searches. The materials used range from wood and bone to plastic and odd scraps of metal. One was fashioned from a toothbrush handle and is still recognisable as such. Many years ago a key was reportedly discovered made from a stiff piece of cardboard. 'Of what use is a key made of cardboard?' I hear you ask. Answer: an inmate trying to escape only needs to use it once!

There are, as you might expect, experts among the prison population to whom most locks present no barrier, which is why prison locks are specially manufactured and guaranteed to be unique in a ratio of several thousand to one. All the same, every lock requires a key and every prisoner is able to observe them several times each day when prison officers lock and unlock cell doors, entrance gates, etc. One man, new to the job, was fumbling with lock and key when a passing inmate cheerfully called 'You've got the wrong key Guv, you want that one!', pointing to another on the bunch.

Would you believe an inmate could make a key out of an odd bit of metal that perfectly matches a prison key, and to a pattern committed to memory, simply by seeing that key in use? It has happened more than once. During training sessions for staff the story is told about a certain prison Governor who habitually waved a key at prisoners when admonishing them. The pattern was memorised and a duplicate was made (and later found). Strict precautions are taken when disposing of unwanted or worn-out keys. At Dartmoor, the pattern is first destroyed by burning with acetylene torches, after which the shanks are buried in concrete to prevent them falling into the wrong hands. The loss of a key or discovery of a duplicate is an extremely serious matter because every lock that key fits has to be changed. In recent years other prisons have had to change hundreds of locks, once, for example, when the imprint of a key was discovered in a piece of pastry hidden in the kitchens, and on another occasion because a duplicate key was found in a cell. On 10th March 1998 the *Daily Mail* reported an incident at Wakefield Prison, Yorkshire, when an inmate was apprehended letting himself back *in* with a skeleton key. He had unlocked three doors and a gate in the security fence, and it was thought he was making a 'dummy run' in preparation for a planned escape when associates would pick him up. In the same year a cell key was lost at Dartmoor and locks had to be changed.

Modern cells have solid metal doors (although there are still a small number of old style wooden ones at Dartmoor) without a handle or locking mechanism on the inside, so escaping from a cell is a rare occurrence. The risk arises when inmates leave their cells to go to exercise or to work. On Boxing Day 1966 five Dartmoor prisoners ganged up on their two supervising officers in the gymnasium, tied them up and stole their keys in order to escape. In his book *The Story of Dartmoor Prison* former Governor Mr. Basil Thomson relates how a warder lost a key in April 1860. A series of escape attempts with a reproduction key took place, and several more were later discovered. 'The trail of the lost key may be traced in the prison records for more than ten years', he wrote. Imagine how often it must have been copied and how many ounces of precious tobacco changed hands among inmates anxious to gain possession of it.

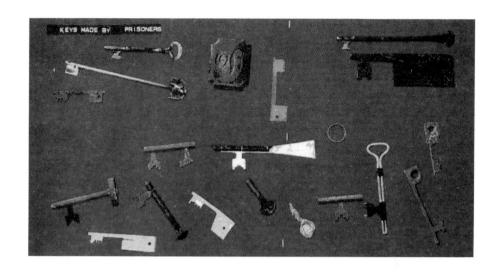

A selection of keys made of metal and wood confiscated during routine cell searches. (Courtesy of Dartmoor Prison Heritage Centre).

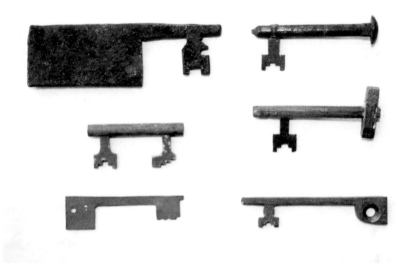

'Of what use is a key made of cardboard?' I hear you ask. Answer: an inmate trying to escape only needs to use it once!

'RUBBER BONES' WEBB

One of the most remarkable and widely remembered escapes from Dartmoor Prison since World War II was that of Harold Roy Webb, better known as 'Rubber Bones'. Despite the fact he was doing time for robbery with violence a cavalier spirit surrounds his exploits. For example he once said to a prison officer escorting him 'We don't need these do we?' handing over his handcuffs after slipping his hands free – it was the sort of thing that earned him his nickname as well as his ability to squeeze his supple body through seemingly impossible apertures. The latter feat, as we shall see, was to gain him immortal fame in the history of Dartmoor.

Webb, a native of Northwich, Cheshire, was sentenced at the Old Bailey in October 1946 to eight years imprisonment and ten strokes of the birch for robbery with violence. He already had a record as an Army deserter and had escaped from military custody more than once. It is perplexing therefore to learn that when he was transferred from Wormwood Scrubs to Dartmoor in June 1947 with twenty four other prisoners, he was the only one in the group who was not manacled to another man like the rest. When they disembarked from the train at Tavistock North Station to board a bus to take them to Princetown he wriggled free of his handcuffs and sprinted away leaving his escorts to ensure the other men were safely accounted for. A passer by some distance away, unaware of the situation, noticed a man climbing a tree and wondered what was going on. It was almost certainly Webb hiding from pursuit until the heat was off.

It took three days to track him down. He was recaptured late one evening near Meldon Quarry, just outside Okehampton almost twelve miles from Tavistock. Webb was a pitiable sight, soaking wet and chilled to the bone, dishevelled and starving. He had survived on berries, chipple onions and the tops of broad beans filched from people's gardens. 'I'm the man you are looking for', he mumbled to the policemen who apprehended him. They were convinced he was a dying man (see *The Hunters and the Hunted*).

With his previous escape record and the more recent escapade to take into consideration he was placed under extra surveillance when he was taken to Dartmoor, in keeping with the rules set out for the 'E' List prisoners (see Authors preface). Yet he accomplished another escape which was to cause a sensation. This time he left by a tunnel, not one he had to dig himself but a man-made one that conducted hot air from the (now obsolete) heating system to each cell. Webb's cell was on the ground floor directly above one of the main ducts. It was during a period employed in the Works Department assisting with repairs that he gained the knowledge he was to use for his escape.

Webb occupied a cell in the bottom row of the large block. The hot air heating system was on the ground level and one of the arched air intakes, now bricked up, can be clearly seen.

His plan and preparations were a masterpiece of cunning, tenacity and, it must be said, sheer guts. His cell was regularly 'turned over' (minutely searched) and at night an officer looked through the 'Judas Hole' of his cell door every half hour. These were just two of the extra precautions taken under 'A' List rules. Imagine if you can the mixture of shock and disbelief when officers entered his cell on the morning of 20th November 1951 and found an improvised 'dummy' under his blankets and no sign of the occupant! Sometime in the night Webb uncovered the entrance he had made to the ventilation and heating shaft to his cell and squirmed his way down to the warm air ducts below. The fresh air intakes, which were flush with the outer wall of the building at ground level, were fitted with bars and on examination it was apparent the fugitive had used a hacksaw blade to weaken them before prising them open. A discarded ladder, a missing pair of gum boots and overalls were further proof he had left the prison.

How on earth was it done? To this day some of the details are unclear but the tale about Webb being inspired by the famous 'Wooden Horse' escape from a prisoner of war camp, related to Dartmoor inmates only two days previously by a visiting speaker, can be discounted. His cell was situated on the floor of 'D' Wing and the concrete floor had a layer of tarmac which he was permitted to keep

These narrow apertures conducted warm air to individual cells. 'Rubber Bones' squeezed his way to freedom down one of these.

polished with black wax. In their excellent book *The Truth About Dartmoor*, two ex-prisoners who were there at the time and knew Webb allege he worked for several months using a stolen chisel and screwdriver to pick away at the floor bit by bit and covering his tracks with thick layers of wax polish. It must have taken weeks to break through the concrete floor and then through the brick wall to the warm air supply duct for his cell (the air entered each cell via a grill which for obvious reasons could not be interfered with). The excavated material was disposed of little by little in the prison yards during exercise periods. The aperture through which he went each night to continue working was covered early each morning by a drawing board he had trimmed carefully so it was an exact fit; the cracks were then filled with wax polish as before. Because of the regular checks made by officers he could only work for a few minutes at a time, so Webb's perseverance and determination were of a rare order.

The time came when he entered the main ducts which directed hot air straight from the furnaces to the various parts of the prison. A visit to these underground tunnels today reveal a complicated system of low passageways, treacherous six foot deep wells, and cloister-like arches which connect to other ducts; it is a dangerous and confusing area to be in even with torches to light

The now redundant main ducts of the warm air heating system.

the way. The whole complex is covered with layers of choking dust which induces violent coughing if disturbed. Imagine going into such a place alone in complete darkness with the sonorous roar of the furnaces and fans blowing searing hot dust-laden air in your face. How to grope your way through this nightmare maze and locate the intakes, then remember the way to and fro', defies the imagination. 'Rubber Bones' Webb did it, to the admiration of his fellow inmates and not a few of the 'screws'.

By the time his absence was reported he was miles away, having located the railway (the now defunct Plymouth – Waterloo main line) and followed it to the little wayside station at Brentor, arriving just in time to board the early morning 'workman train' to Exeter. Every risky endeavour requires a lot of luck to succeed and 'Rubber Bones' enjoyed more than his share of luck that day. Mr. 'Jimmy' Osborne, station master, ticket collector, signalman and clerk ran Brentor station single – handed and knew every regular passenger by sight and most of them by name. He was on holiday otherwise the game would have ended there and then for Webb. Then there was the guard to contend with but dressed as he was in overalls and gumboots he mingled with the workmen and was allowed to board without a ticket and without question saying 'I'm working up the line', giving the impression he belonged to the gang of railwaymen and quarry workers already on the train The regular guard was also on leave and the one on the train that day was a temporary replacement—how lucky can you get?

As the train neared Exeter Webb jumped off and continued his journey by road, hitching lifts to London. On arrival however it dawned on him that having accomplished an exceptional feat of daring and endurance his predicament now was precarious to say the least. In short he had no friends in the city who could help him and he had nowhere to go for food and shelter. He never considered going to his home in Northwich because he knew it would be under police surveillance day and night. For the same reason he didn't consider going to Cardiff where his girl friend lived and who was also being watched. Probably in desperation he had risked asking for help at an address in Hackney, letting slip that he was an escapee from Dartmoor Prison. Scotland Yard soon got hold of this information and accordingly the hunt for him was called off in Devon and concentrated in the capital. With the newspapers keeping track of latest developments and a national hue and cry out for him he wandered around London unrecognized for a week, living rough and sleeping under the barrows left overnight by the 'barrow boys' in a cul-de-sac known as John Bull Yard but which was in fact the rear of 151 Oxford Street. His food consisted of left over fruit and vegetables, some of it rotten and his bed was the hard packed freezing cold ground in the yard.

It was in these dismal surroundings the saga ended. A plain clothes policeman happened to spot Webb as he entered the yard on Saturday 25th November and recognized him. Within minutes a team of C.I.D. officers arrived, led by Chief Inspector Forbes Leith. When challenged Webb gave up without a struggle saying 'I'm glad it's all over'. The ordeal had taken its toll and it showed in his gaunt unshaven features to the extent few people would have recognized him from the description or photos of him that were circulated.

Thus ended one of the biggest manhunts ever launched with more than 8,000 police officers involved altogether. When he was recaptured he had been on the run for five days, short of food and money, sleeping in the open without adequate clothing, and undergoing who knows what stress wondering how much longer he could remain at large before being retaken. The policemen took him to Savile Row and gave him his first hot meal since he left the Moor. After spending the night at Wandsworth Prison he was taken back to Dartmoor where, sad to say, his former admirers now treated him with scorn for giving up so easily (so they thought). As it happened it was not the last prison sentence Webb served nor was it his last escape, but for the rest of his life he was remembered (and still is at Dartmoor) as an exceptionally brave man in his own right.

Webb's prison block and the wall he scaled to freedom.

VIOLENCE, GLAMOUR, AND PUNISHMENTS

Prison escapes have, in the past, often been regarded as some kind of sporting event by members of the public who frequently gave recaptured prisoners an ovation similar to that directed at many television and 'pop' idols today. An extreme case was that of two escaped convicts who were cornered at South Tawton, near Okehampton, in 1851. A farmer and his son assisted the local Constable in capturing them and were badly injured in the struggle, the farmer being severely kicked and beaten. The Constable suffered head injuries after being hit with a stone tied in a handkerchief. All three men then had to fight off the populace, who had sided with the runaways and plied them with tobacco and beer. One of the convicts was quite drunk when he was finally secured. Dartmoor Prison's evil reputation was then in the making, which probably accounted for the inhabitants sympathising with the fugitives.

The Reverend Clifford Rickards in *A Prison Chaplain on Dartmoor* tells how several prisoners got away from a farm party near the prison, only to be recaptured almost at once. They were marched back through Princetown to the prison. Shouts of 'They've got them!' and 'Here they come', attracted the Reverend into the street in time to see a huge crowd of residents and visitors surrounding a group of warders escorting the escapees back to jail. Loud cheering and shouts of encouragement rang out, to the delight of the prisoners who laughed back at them and appeared to be having the time of their lives. Reverend Rickards then relates another side of the story: further up the street a group of anxious women had gathered, all of them warders' wives. 'It's no laughing matter for us', they said, 'it's our husbands who will be made to suffer when the enquiry is made'. And so it was: the warders, who were invariably held responsible for escapes, were fined or demoted for neglect of duty.

A similar, but less 'glamorous' episode, took place in 1879, and the excitement of the chase, together with the subsequent treatment of the recaptured men, was vividly portrayed by a convict who was present at the scene. He described the event in a letter smuggled out of Dartmoor to a prison acquaintance who had completed his sentence. The instigator of the escape attempt was a prisoner named Morgan who had run away once before, and was obviously an 'opportunist' hell - bent on making a getaway. (Taken from *Convict Life* by Ticket of Leave Man, Wyman & Sons 1879).

The day's work was done and the farm party had stacked their rakes, forks and other tools before going to collect their hats and coats, which had been left beside a hedge some distance away. 'Now's our chance!' cried Morgan, and eight men disappeared over the hedge in a trice, 'leaving their guards open mouthed and decidedly off their guard. But of their escape there was no fear', the letter said, 'thirty or forty Devonshire labourers had heard the alarm whistle and the signal gun. They were soon joined by others and in strong parties started in pursuit. I think I may safely say that for the reward for each capture there will be at least half a dozen claimants.' (A reward of £5 was payable for apprehending an escapee.)

Meanwhile the rest of the party were marched back to the prison, passing on the way 'an excited, pale faced youth, flourishing a double barrelled shotgun in a most alarming manner, exclaiming "Which way have they gone, who will I shoot?" He has been the butt of a good many jokes since, for it was discovered when the time came to shoot he had left his ammunition pouch at his quarters!'

It being a perfectly clear evening with visibility of at least twenty miles, the fugitives were quickly rounded up. 'Last Friday', the letter went on, 'Director Morrish came down to Dartmoor redolent with the odour of Whitehall and armed with all the majesty of a Supreme Judge. Five of the men received two dozen each with the 'cat' and the other three were birched. I saw the runaways this morning in their yellow dresses,* they are breaking stones.' As for the warders, the account concludes: 'This morning the Governor received from Parliament–Street the decision of the Directors as to the punishment of the officers who were in charge. They are each fined ten shillings and reduced to Probation Class for three months, so their pay will be reduced for that period.'

The narrative closes on a touching note: 'And now our old friend will have to curtail the number of his visits to the 'Spotted Dog'.

* Yellow clothing worn by recaptured escapees.

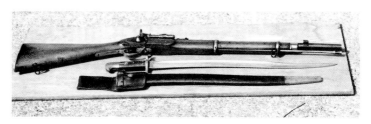

Snider Carbine with bayonet and sheath. Standard issue from 1866 to guards and warders of outside work parties. Discontinued in the 1950s. (Photo courtesy of Prison Officer Nick Fletcher).

'JUMBO' PARSONS

In most prisons sooner or later an incident will occur that is not only memorable and unusual but beggars belief for audacity. The last chapter of this book relates just such a case, the story of how and why ex-convict Joe Denny broke **into** Dartmoor Prison after being released. Incredibly the feat was repeated more than seventy years later by criminals intent on 'rescuing' one of their kind – namely Charles Arthur Dennis Parsons.

Charles 'Jumbo' Parsons, as his nickname suggests, was a big man who stood well over six foot tall and was built like the proverbial barn door. He was also a dangerous and violent criminal who was sentenced to seven years imprisonment for robbery with violence at the Central Criminal Court on 29th January 1957. The proceeds of the robbery were never recovered.

Parsons turned up in Devon with his wife whilst 'on the run', having escaped from prison. They stayed for just a few days at a time at various caravan sites, trying to keep ahead of the Metropolitan Police 'Flying Squad' who were actively pursuing them. The 'Squad' men were aware their quarry had been known to carry a revolver (a much less common occurrence in the 1950s) and were anxious to put him back behind bars where he could do no harm.

The Parsons' mistake was to have parcels sent 'Care of the G.P.O.' which they collected from the local post offices wherever they happened to be. It is a reasonable assumption that the packages contained money from the proceeds of the robbery with which to fund their escapade. It can also be concluded they had very trustworthy friends or relatives assisting them. In October 1957 the police officers following their trail decided to concentrate on the Torbay area and the numerous caravan sites there, not forgetting the main post office which was kept under continuous surveillance. True to form Mrs. Parsons called to collect a parcel and was followed by the officers to Paignton and thence to a caravan site at Goodrington. Policemen and dog handlers from Torquay and Paignton assembled at 7.00 pm that same day and quietly surrounded the caravan Mrs. Parsons had been seen to enter. They knocked at the door and when it was opened they burst in to find 'Jumbo' with his hat and coat on and his bags packed ready to depart. They were in the nick of time and for Parsons the game was up. He was returned to prison and later transferred to Dartmoor.

A year later, on Monday 13th October 1958, there was a flurry of police activity at Dartmoor when evidence of a planned escape was discovered in the prison quarry. A prison officer found a revolver and a note hidden among some rocks together with a toilet bag which contained money, a rough map of the area, and two driving licences with certificates of insurance. The map indicated a wood known locally as 'Long Plantation' where a car had been left and on investigation a fairly new black Austin A.55 was found with the ignition key in the switch and ample petrol in the tank. It was later established the vehicle bore false number plates and the documents mentioned had been stolen in London days before. Two sports jackets, trousers and a shirt were in the boot. It was obvious an escape was to take place by a prisoner with ample funds and the help of well-paid accomplices and/or loyal family members. This ambitious plan had now been foiled and there must have been much grinding of teeth by a certain Dartmoor Prison inmate, the most likely person being 'Jumbo' Parsons who was in residence on the moor.

The events that took place just seven months later were not only astonishing in their boldness but were similar in several respects to those just related and what is more, were proved to be related to inmate Parsons.

At about 2.00 am on the night of 18th May 1959 a Dartmoor Prison officer happened to glance out of the third floor window where he was standing and was flabbergasted when he saw a man in civilian clothing stroll across the prison yard inside the boundary walls. The October 1958 incident was fresh in the minds of every member of staff and the officer therefore wasted no time in contacting the Principle Officer on duty in the Orderly Room who at once organised a search for the intruder. He himself took part and by chance came across a man crouching against a partly demolished wall who immediately ran off shouting 'Get away! Get away!' which was (rightly) interpreted by his pursuer as a warning to partners in

A mounted officer in front of 'D' wing (now 'G' wing). Parsons' would-be rescuer, Ward, went in over the wall seen through the gateway. (Courtesy of Dartmoor Prison Heritage Centre).

crime. The man was caught and was recognised to be Edward Charles Ward who had not only been released from Dartmoor just days before but had occupied a cell in the very prison wing that housed 'Jumbo' Parsons. Ward admitted breaking into the prison using a discarded scaffold pole to scale the boundary wall and that the purpose of his 'visit' was to bring in a quantity of 'snout' (prison slang for tobacco). It was realised that Ward was almost certainly not alone, having called out repeated warnings whilst being chased and a full alarm was raised. The Princetown Police Constable was informed who in turn would have telephoned Police Headquarters in Exeter. Things then moved quickly as the Deputy Governor supervised a hunt outside the prison for Ward's accomplices. Two men were disturbed in the vicinity of the American Cemetery (the burial ground for American prisoners of war captured in the War of 1812) who fled in the direction of 'Long Plantation' which lies about a mile from the prison in the Two Bridges direction.

The Princetown Constable made his way to 'Long Plantation' where he discovered a Ford Consul motor car with false number plates, afterwards found to have been stolen in Middlesex. The engine was still warm. Meanwhile Detective Sergeant C.J.Tarr arrived from Plympton and after talking with Ward went to the prison yard where he found the scaffold pole with a length of rope attached which had been used to gain entry. The most significant find was a large car jack and a sledge hammer close to the ground floor cell occupied by Parsons. There can be no doubt as to the use these would have been put if Ward had not been detected.

What about the two men who had been seen running away from the Deputy Governor's search party? As part of the police procedures a Motor Patrol Constable was in the vicinity of Moretonhampstead when at 3.20 am he passed a car travelling in the opposite direction towards Exeter. It was a Ford Zodiac containing two men and the police driver's suspicions were at once aroused. Not being able to stop this vehicle he reported the incident and every police force in the westcountry was alerted. The car was intercepted and stopped two hours later on the A30 main road to London near Yeovil. The occupants were two well-known criminals, twenty three year old John William Hayes of Hillingdon, Middlesex and Benjamin Hiller, thirty three, from Tooting, London. They were taken to Yeovil Police Station and detained for questioning.

Detective Sergeant Tarr travelled up from Devon to interview Hiller and Hayes who admitted having been in the Moretonhampstead area only because they had got lost returning from Torquay. They both denied knowing Ward but a search of the two men, their vehicle and belongings revealed damning evidence to the contrary. When Hayes was searched two car parking tickets and three cinema tickets were found – all originating from Newton Abbot. It was more than likely that Ward was the third man to visit the cinema and had driven the second car, the one found at

Long Plantation for the escape. In the Zodiac was a suitcase containing shoes size 10½ and a suit to fit a man more than six feet tall, all intended for 'Jumbo' Parsons no doubt, but how to prove it?

To begin with Hiller said the clothing was his but as he was only 5 foot 8 inches tall and his companion Hayes was of smaller stature it was obviously untrue and both men were taken back to Devon to be remanded in custody. It was at this point that meticulous examination of the suit was rewarded. Not only was it a perfect fit for Parsons but when the pockets were turned inside out the wallet section in the jacket revealed a tailor's trade tag which was not visible unless the lining was fully exposed. As well as a reference number the tag bore the words '14th April 1956 – C.A.Parsons'. This evidence and enquiries at the (London) tailors, together with recognition of the three men by staff at the Newton Abbot cinema was a crucial part of the total proof with which to charge the three men as follows:

1. Jointly and feloniously conveying a sledge hammer, a car jack and rope into H.M.Prison, Dartmoor with intent to facilitate the escape of a prisoner there confined.

2. Conspiracy.

Hayes was further charged with stealing the car from Middlesex.

At Devon Quarter Sessions held on 3rd July 1959 Ward, Hayes and Hiller, all known criminals, were each sentenced to two years imprisonment on both charges, the sentences to run concurrently. Hayes was awarded an additional two years for larceny of the car. Their pal 'Jumbo' Parsons remained in his Dartmoor cell.

'Jumbo' Parsons was held in the large wing, left of centre. The American Cemetery is situated in the wooded area behind.

THE HUNTERS AND THE HUNTED

The task of searching for escaped prisoners has always rested with the police force. Prison warders worked closely with the police, manning road blocks and assisting in searches as directed by them, but if the escapees were still at large three days later, they were recalled to run the prison and the local constabulary assumed sole responsibility.

Prior to 1966 Dartmoor Prison did not have radio communications, a dog section, or an internal security fence. In addition there was a more dangerous and desperate type of criminal interned there, many of them serving long sentences and therefore highly motivated toward escaping. Nearly every escapee who did abscond did so in the winter when the weather was at its worst or under cover of mist and the long nights. Those engaged in looking for them faced almost unbearable hardships, turning out at a moment's notice (the Tavistock Police abandoned their annual Christmas Dinner on one occasion) to face long hours manning isolated checkpoints or tramping over the moors, perhaps in torrents of rain, sleet, or snow, with icy winds that cut through their uniforms (there was no special protective clothing issued). It was worse for the fugitives, who were even less adequately clad, and unsure of their whereabouts. Policemen long retired have a fund of horror stories about their experiences, some of which would be held in doubt had they been told by someone other than a trusted 'Bobby'. On one occasion two escapees were found by police cowering in the snow,

Police check point 1930s. (Courtesy of David German).

half-frozen, and actually crying with pain in the cold. Another prisoner, desperate for food, tore the leg off a dead sheep and ate the raw meat; yet another consumed some candles he found in an abandoned farmhouse where he took shelter.

For the hunters there was no shelter. Policemen were posted to lonely cross-roads and bridges to maintain a vigil for as long as was necessary, perhaps several days, and were expected to remain there until relieved. These duties were often shared by prison warders, but there were times when the police had to go it alone. One old-timer, Mr. Ken Northey of Tavistock, recalls spending fourteen hours at Moorshop on the edge of Dartmoor, in the dark, in a snowstorm, alone and without refreshment. By morning he was so cold he sought the meagre shelter of the nearest ditch and kept watch from there. He had to face the uncompromising wrath of his Inspector when he turned up next morning. Another policeman was manning a bridge overlooking the railway on the outskirts of Tavistock. After enduring a cold, lonely night, and with snow falling, he was delighted when, in the morning, a baker's van delivering freshly made pasties to Tavistock, stopped and the driver offered him one. When he looked inside he discovered his 'hot fresh pasties' were frozen and covered in a layer of snow that had penetrated the cracks in the doors. Nevertheless, with commendable determination, a ravenous constable managed to find a palatable pasty at the bottom of the pile.

The popular notion of officers chasing fugitives over the moors in a mist with bloodhounds straining at the leash is only partly true. Neither the prison nor the police had bloodhounds to employ, but there were at least two generous sources from which help came from time to time. In the 1920s a Miss Lowe of Minions, near Liskeard, Cornwall, loaned three hounds to help police and warders hunt down two desperate escapees. They were directed and controlled by a Miss Clarke, and although they were not directly responsible for recapturing the two men, the dogs proved invaluable in guiding search parties all the way from Princetown to Roborough Down in driving wind and rain along the very route they'd taken, as was proved by the discovery of their discarded prison clothing. Both men were later apprehended in Plymouth.

From 1946 until 1953 assistance was freely given by Mrs. H.M. Blakiston of Bratton Tor Kennels, Bratton Clovelly (and later of Lydford) who bred bloodhounds. This lady knew, as did Miss Lowe and Miss Clarke before her, that hounds only worked to advantage under the direction of their owners; consequently she accompanied the police on many occasions, sometimes across rough country, often at night and in bad weather. A former traffic policeman, Mr.R. Borlase, recalls sending a car to Bratton Clovelly to collect bloodhounds and the resident Constable, the late Mr.J. Gater, immediately the force was informed a prisoner was at large. P.C. Gater got to know the dogs well and became proficient in handling them himself, especially a hound named 'Turpin'. Mrs. Blakiston had paid seventy five guineas for him and trained him herself specially for tracking.

Hunting an escaped prisoner. P.C. Joe Gater and bloodhound Turpin followed by P.C. Reg Borlase.

It was P.C. Joe Gater who, with P.C. Brian Kendrick, was responsible for forming the Devon Constabulary dog unit in the late 1950s, based in Torquay. In 1964, the unit was extended to other stations, including Tavistock. They used Alsatians who could not only track, but were capable of apprehending an escapee until their handlers caught up with them. Dartmoor Prison followed suit on the recommendation of the Mountbatten Enquiry after Frank Mitchell's escape in 1966. Police dogs, with their handlers, manned the prison for several months to enable prison officers and dogs to be trained. The prison dog section today plays a prominent role in drugs detection with its sniffer dogs.

For more than sixty years the Devon Police have worked to guidelines set out in an 'Escape Scheme' devised by a remarkable man, Major Lyndon Henry Morris, C.B.E., M.C., D.L. He was the Governor of Dartmoor Prison (the youngest ever to hold that position) prior to taking up the post of Chief Constable of Devon on 2nd. April 1931 He was therefore well qualified to organise a system that has been successful for so long and with amendments, is still in use today. For security reasons the details cannot be revealed except to say the plan involved sealing off the moor, setting up roadside check points, and directing search parties from a

Central Control Room. Police helicopters are an essential part of every escape operation today.

A convict hunt used to be the only occasion when policemen could claim overtime, after all available resources and the Special Constabulary had been mobilised. The 'Specials' were, and are, a voluntary force, but no less enthusiastic for that. The author remembers one Special Constable – his father-in-law, the late Mr.E.J. Batten of Brentor – spending many a cold winter night keeping watch on the railway lines at Brentor station, turning out after working all day and going to work as usual the next day. 'Rubber Bones' Webb (see page 27), boarded a train at Brentor station and got clear of the county. By tradition the policeman who actually caught an escaped prisoner had the privilege of returning him to Dartmoor and on at least one occasion it was a 'Special' who did the honours.

One might think that after all the inconveniences and privations endured in order to capture them, prisoners would receive little sympathy from their captors. In fact the opposite has been the case. The pitiful condition some escapees have been found in has aroused the finest instincts in the policemen involved, who are on record as having had a 'whip-round' at the station to nip along to the nearest cafe or fish and chip shop to buy a hot meal for a starving prisoner. Others have been plied with sandwiches and endless mugs of tea whilst cheerful banter was often exchanged in the aftermath of a successful 'hunt'. I quote the words of an 'old lag' ('Rubber Bones', writing in *The People* Sunday newspaper after his release from prison) who was recaptured near Okehampton wet through, starving, and exhausted, after three days on the run in freezing November weather: "After my capture kind arms took hold of me, the arms of the Devon Constabulary. 'Poor devil' said one. 'He must be nearly dead' said another. Then I found a paper bag full of cakes in one hand and an orange in the other, whilst a cigarette was being thrust in my mouth and someone else was lighting it. I'll never forget those grand, fine policemen." After describing being taken to Tavistock police station, he concluded: "I did not stay long in that dream world. Very soon two warders arrived from Dartmoor Prison". All of which sums up very well the (usually) inevitable conclusion to a Dartmoor escape.

LOW RISK PRISONERS — CAN YOU EVER BE SURE ?

Category 'C' prisoners are not a high escape or security risk, but may be 'opportunists'.

Category 'D' prisoners represent no risk whatsoever either of escaping or being a threat to the public.

Dartmoor Prison farm closed in 2004. With its demise there ended a long history of success when prize cattle, sheep and horses were bred and the enclosed areas of the surrounding moor were transformed into productive farmland. This was a part of the original conditions under which the Duchy of Cornwall leased the land to the prison authorities and it was highly labour intensive. In recent years the farm proper was a popular workplace with prisoners, the one essential requirement being they had to be Category 'C' or 'D'.

It was October 1973 when the farm foreman, Mr. D. Kennelly, took two inmates to do some repair work to the prison leat, a four mile long shallow waterway which at that time extracted water from the River Walkham to supply the prison. The two men with him were thirty seven year old Peter Frost, serving six years for burglary and twenty nine year old George Peart, also serving six years for theft and forgery. Both men were low category prisoners and they were both due for release within weeks so anyone would have felt safe and at ease in their company.

Mr. Kennelly drove them to their place of work in the prison van and on the way back he decided to check a cowshed on another part of the farm. All three entered the shed where, without warning, the foreman was viciously attacked and overpowered. He was trussed with sisal cord and tape around his ankles and knees; his wrists were also tied behind his back with cord and tape. Finally they put a cloth over his head and taped it over his mouth to prevent him calling for help. For good measure they then tied him to a water trough in the shed and left him, making their escape in the van – an Austin 'Gypsy'.

It took Mr. Kennelly two hours of frantic struggling to get free from the trough by which time the escapees had driven to Bishopsteignton near Teignmouth in south Devon and abandoned the van in a copse. The prison had not an inkling that anything was amiss and the fugitives had more than a head start in their flight. On Dartmoor a thick mist with drizzle had descended when, still bound and gagged, their victim managed to roll and crawl across a field to the Rundlestone – Two Bridges road, a remarkable feat for a man who had been savagely beaten and tied up. Sadly three drivers ignored the sight of a man lying helpless at the side of the road but at last two holidaymakers, Mr. and Mrs. T. Wilcocks of Eastbourne, pulled up and freed him. After being taken to the prison by his rescuers and raising the alarm Mr. Kennelly was admitted to the prison hospital for treatment to his wounds.

The abandoned prison van was later discovered by a farmer, Mr. G. Webber who notified the police. They at once attended the scene with tracker dogs but with the escapees having several hours head start of their pursuers it was a hopeless task to trace them. By now they were almost certainly out of the county but the hunt for them continued relentlessly and they were finally located in London. Frost made no resistance on being arrested. Peart put up a fight when he was found on a building site in the capital but was restrained and both men were returned to Devon to await trial for their misdeeds.

They appeared before Mr. Justice Bristow in January 1973 at Bodmin Crown Court on three charges:

1. Escaping from Dartmoor Prison.
2. Taking a vehicle without consent.
3. Causing bodily harm to Mr. Kennelly.

The only mitigating factor in Frost's case was that he had surrendered peacefully when arrested. Peart on the other hand had strongly resisted arrest. His counsel suggested only sufficient violence had been used in the attack on Mr. Kennelly to ensure an escape and that the attack itself had not been a vicious one! It was in all probability the only mitigating circumstance which could be put forward but it was dismissed by the Judge. Both men had an extra eighteen months added to their existing sentences.

The farm foreman was the victim of an opportunist escape and a betrayal of the trust that went with a Category 'C' and 'D' designation. The ruthless handling he received at the hands of these two individuals resulted in him being invalided out of the Prison Service at only thirty years of age.

Dartmoor Prison Heritage Centre curators, Laura Worth and Dave Francis, display a grapnel, confiscated in 2004 from a Category 'C' inmate.

THE FRENCH AT DARTMOOR

Every prison has a high wall around it and Dartmoor had two such walls when it opened as a French Prisoner of War Depot in 1809 (see page 3). The inner wall had platforms for the soldier guards who kept watch over the interior and who didn't hesitate to shoot or bayonet anyone trying to escape. Most of the prisoners in those early days were sailors, among them crews of privateers, vicious desperadoes who would stop at nothing in an effort to escape. Under cover of darkness, mist, or heavy rain, many a man, sometimes groups of men, found a way of scaling the boundary walls undetected. This was an achievement in itself, because there were wires strung around the walls with bells suspended from them. If the wire was disturbed, the jangling of the bells was the signal for Drummers to beat 'To Arms'. Then every guard, on or off duty, armed himself and rushed to apprehend the escapees. The ruthlessness with which this was done is illustrated in the following incident.

French Prisoners of War marching to Dartmoor Prison under escort. (From an oil painting by an unknown inmate).

In 1810 the Nottinghamshire Militia arrived at Dartmoor and several French prisoners, seeking to take advantage of the new arrival's supposed lack of vigilance on their first night on guard duty, attempted a mass escape, but were detected milling about in the area between the two walls known as the 'Military Walk'. When the alarm was given, every militiaman, some half-clothed, ran to the scene, and in the confusion one of their own men, who hadn't had time to put on his uniform and was mistaken for a prisoner, was stabbed to death by bayonet thrusts.

A Dartmoor prisoner of war attempting to escape not only had the stone walls, alarm bells, and armed sentries to contend with. There was the moor to cross, without signposts and a population ranged against him, either for fear of punishment if they helped him, or the possibility of a £5 reward if they turned him in. The tors and bogs made travel difficult and there was little shelter. Besides, a man needed rest, food and the means of crossing the Channel. Torbay was usually their objective, where there was a chance of stealing a boat, or maybe persuading a fisherman to take them to France (fishermen on both sides were, by mutual agreement, immune from hostilities during the French wars). Occasionally boats and their occupants were 'hijacked' and forced to sail to France under threat of death. Eventually things got so bad the Admiralty ordered all unattended vessels on the south coast to have their oars and sails removed as a precaution against theft by escaping prisoners of war.

Smugglers were involved in the escape trade and 'trade' is precisely what developed when professional 'escape agents' began to appear. These men were unscrupulous scallywags who would arrange everything for an escapee — for a price. Lucky customers were whisked away to somewhere safe, perhaps an isolated house or a quiet inn with an understanding (and equally expensive) landlord who would arrange transportation to France. Sometimes things went tragically wrong though. On 26th January 1811, five French officers living on parole at Moretonhampstead stole away from their lodgings after dark and met a local carrier, Richard Tapper, who had horses waiting to take them to Topsham on the River Exe near Exeter. There they were joined by two well known smugglers from Cheriton Bishop, brothers Thomas and William Vinnicombe who, for a down payment of £25 and the promise of another £250, took them on board their boat and set sail down the river for France. At the mouth of the river their luck ran out when the vessel ran aground off Exmouth and they were caught. The French officers, three of whom were ship's captains, were sent to Plymouth, probably to Mill Prison. Tapper and the Vinnicombes were tried at the Devon Assizes in the summer of 1812 and sentenced to transportation for life.

At Dartmoor a number of prisoners were employed outside the prison on road making and various building projects that included the Church and Parsonage. They were paid sixpence a day, but as reported by the Americans who took over when the French war ended, payment was made every three months and not at all if there was an escape during that period. That didn't stop determined men. One bold Frenchman effected a unique method of escape when his colleagues encased him in a recess in the chimney they were constructing in the Parsonage and walled him in, leaving air holes in loose mortar and successfully concealing his absence at roll call. The prisoner waited until they departed at the end of the day, forced his way out (the mortar not having had time to set) and made his getaway. The question might be asked: what motivated his companions, knowing they faced certain punishment when he was found to be missing?

As already mentioned, heavy penalties were inflicted on sentries who aided escapees. In addition, a barrier of iron railings inside the inner wall prevented prisoners from approaching the guards and fraternising with them and maybe bribing them for help in escaping. It did no good because several instances of bribery came to light as well as an unknown number that did not. In 1812 three French prisoners paid a Roscommons Militiaman £2, the going rate at the time, to help them 'over the wall'. Paddy wasn't the only one among the rank and file who had no scruples about supplementing his pay in this manner. Soldiers were poorly paid and conscripted from the lowest classes, drunkards almost to a man, so it was no surprise to find so many of them willing to risk a flogging, or perhaps their lives, for the price of a drink. There was a sting in the tail though; the Irishman was detected trying to pass forged notes, the price of his treachery, at the daily market that was held within the prison. Forgery was a big problem in every prisoner of war depot and the death penalty had been introduced to try and stop it. The forger, a prisoner called Lustique, was later identified and both he and the soldier were tried and hanged.

On a lighter note, the best known story is that of *Le Capitaine Calonne et sa Dame* — the title of a play performed by the prisoners. Theatricals were a prominent feature of prison life and performances were often attended by the British. On this occasion a certain officer and his wife generously offered to help by lending the leading actors a uniform and female clothing. The offer was gladly accepted and the performance was a huge success until, towards the end, an announcement was made: 'Messieurs, the Captain and his wife have left the prison'. The implication was clear and only too true — the French 'Captain and his wife' had passed unchallenged out of the main prison entrance to freedom, leaving an embarrassed officer and his lady having to endure hoots and whistles of derision from a delighted prisoner audience!

THE CAPTURE OF 'RUBY' SPARKS

What was one of the most astonishing convict related incidents of all time happened in London in 1940. Among Dartmoor Prison's most notorious inmates was John Charles 'Ruby' Sparks, a well known criminal specialising in 'smash and grab' robberies and burglary. Army deserter and ringleader in Dartmoor's famous mutiny in 1932, Sparks escaped from the moorland jail in January 1940 and was at large for 170 days – an all-time record made possible largely by the wartime 'blackout'. In August that year he was traced to an address in North London and four 'Flying Squad' detectives went there and arrested him. At the Station their suspect (naturally) protested his innocence and persisted in wearing the dark glasses he had on when apprehended. The Squad men had a problem because they had acted on information received without any direct evidence with which to charge him or indeed take his fingerprints. Everything hinged on getting Sparks to admit his true identity. Three of the team knew Sparks but could not be certain they had their man. The fourth man was Detective Sergeant Matthew Brinnand, only recently promoted and retained on the Squad (the ususal practice was to be transferred after being promoted). He was obviously highly thought of by his commanding officers and their confidence in him was about to be justified in a remarkable manner. His three colleagues who were acquainted with Sparks debated for a quarter of an hour and decided they had to let him go. Brinnand disagreed and said if he was released he personally would arrest him the moment he set foot outside. There was an argument lasting another ten minutes but Brinnand was adamant. 'That man is Sparks!' he declared 'let him go if you want but if you do I will arrest him on the pavement outside'.

The detainee listened to all this with mounting anger and finally lost his composure, smashing his dark glasses on the floor and cursing Det. Sgt. Brinnand. Thus ended the most lengthy escape by a prisoner from Dartmoor Prison. Did Matthew Brinnand have a 'gut feeling' about Sparks or was it a clever ploy designed to make their man lose his temper the way he did and admit his identity? Which ever it was the fugitive realised the game was up and it had all been for nothing – the sequel to practically every escape attempt on record.

Footnote

This remarkable man was a mixture of good and bad. During the 1932 mutiny at Dartmoor Prison, Sparks saved a warder from assault and possibly being murdered. When World War II broke out he volunteered for the British Army but during a forty eight hour leave period got into trouble over forged ration books. At his trial his Commanding Officer gave a character reference for him saying he was a fine soldier and didn't want to lose him. It did no good and 'Ruby' was sent back to Dartmoor. Like so many others he took a wrong path in life otherwise he might have been a credit to society.

A BRIEF TASTE OF FREEDOM

It was a glorious sunny day during June 1924, which attracted many visitors to Princetown. Most of them had come to see the prison and the convict working parties who were a common feature on the moor in those days. One had only to go along the Rundlestone – Two Bridges road to observe the farm parties at work and in the town itself, if you were lucky, at the right time of day you got a close up view of armed guards escorting prisoners to and from their place of work. There was a curious fascination about the prison and its inmates which persists to the present day.

A drama was about to be enacted which took sightseers and moor lovers alike by surprise and gave them a tale to tell for years to come. Around 300 convicts who were haymaking in a prison farm field known as Park Corner had just stopped for a lunch break. It was a peaceful scene: the convicts sat in the shade of a stone wall eating their dinners of pea soup, potatoes and bread out of round prison dinner cans (a four wheeled cart brought their dinners from the prison); half the number of warders in charge were also having their dinner, sitting in a group in the middle of the field whilst their comrades kept watch until their turn to eat. Suddenly there was a whistle blast sounding an alarm — seven prisoners had made a dash for freedom. Over the hedge they sped and scattered, pursued by mounted warders armed with pistols. When one of them opened fire two of the fugitives were wounded; the remaining five ran for dear life, discarding their prison issue boots with the imprint of the famous 'broad arrow' nailed into the soles which would leave an unmistakable trail to be followed. One man shed his breeches and belt as well to allow the maximum freedom of movement in his flight leaving him clad with just his shirt and underwear.

The remaining convicts formed two files and were escorted back to the prison. One warder ran to a nearby telegraph pole where there was a field telephone communicating with the watch tower adjacent to the prison quarry where watchers could observe most of the farm land. Within minutes the surrounding countryside was overrun by uniformed officers speeding to their appointed locations. They would maintain a lookout for any sign of the missing men, some with binoculars and others with firearms, all of them intent on containing the runaways within a cordon. All traffic on the moor was halted at roadblocks and the drivers questioned, in the hope they may have seen suspicious looking people during their journey and be able to pinpoint possible areas to extend the searches. A watch had to be kept also on unattended motor cars left at the roadside by picnickers, an additional task but a necessary one because all the escapees could drive. All adjacent police forces were informed of the escapes together with descriptions of the missing men and immediate assistance was given by the Plymouth City Police under Chief

Constable H. Sanders who arranged for checkpoints to be established at key points around the moor. Answering questions from reporters arriving at the scene the Prison Governor, Major F. Morgan, commented: 'They are inside a ring. It is only a matter of closing in on them', adding 'we have got no lambs here, they are all old hands'. Warders engaged in the hunt were more forthright, describing three of them as highly dangerous individuals.

It was not a good day for absconding from prison. The brilliant sunshine and clear skies made for excellent visibility on Dartmoor and that, together with the large number of visitors present, some of whom enthusiastically joined in the search, meant that the convicts' time at large would be very limited. In fact for two of the men their 'liberty' lasted a mere twenty minutes. Constable Kelleway the resident Princetown policeman was informed that loud whistles (a recognised alarm signal) were heard near the Oakery, a little dell between Princetown and Two Bridges. He at once got on his bicycle and met the warders who had seen the escapees and told him which way they had gone.

The old signal station above the Prison quarry. Only the foundations remain today. (Courtesy of Prison Officer Mike Chamberlain).

At a point nearer to Two Bridges he left his bike and legged it across the moor, catching sight of two of the men almost at once heading towards Bachelors Hall. He caught up with and restrained a convict named Ray whilst the other man by the name of Cox got away by jumping over the nearby leat only to meet up with a search party and recaptured.

Already hundreds of excited sightseers had congregated in an almost festive mood, a trait most certainly not shared by prison staff faced with the responsibility of hunting the escapees. For those who were in charge of the haymaking party, there was the unpleasant prospect of disciplinary charges being brought against them for negligence. The visitors who managed to catch sight of the recaptured men described them in over-dramatised terms such as (from a motorist): 'I did not notice them very closely because I was more concerned with avoiding them – they looked very fierce', and from a bystander: 'He was a fierce looking brute with a murderous expression'. All of which no doubt held their listeners spellbound in the days ahead.

Out on the moor the warders continued the hunt relentlessly, some on horseback others on foot, covering a wide sweep towards the Yelverton – Plymouth area where their quarry was last seen heading. At 5.00 pm their attention was drawn to a wet morass where one of the dogs accompanying them was acting in an agitated manner. On investigation they found one of the convicts immersed up to his neck in the watery mire in an attempt at concealment. He was physically weary and

Mounted patrol.

easily taken into custody just as his companion, who had been hiding close by tried to run off. He too was easily caught and the two men, whose names were Myers and Ford, were taken back to the prison.

It was around 7.30 pm before the fifth and last man was recaptured on the moor in the direction of Yelverton. He was called Evans and it was he who had shed his clothing as well as his boots, which was a foolish thing to do even on a Dartmoor summer day. By the time he was recaptured he was not only hungry and exhausted but was beginning to suffer from the cold that creeps over the high moorland near to dusk. He would certainly have ended up a sick man from exposure if he had not been discovered before nightfall.

It had been a day of assorted events. The seven runaways, two of whom it will be remembered were nursing wounds, learned a harsh lesson in their futile effort to escape and would be punished for their efforts. Their colleagues in the prison, who were locked up whilst the hunt was in progress, were sure to give them a hard time as a result. The warders in charge of that particular farm party awaited the reprimands that would inevitably follow an inquiry. The holidaymakers and local residents had an entertaining afternoon and the newspapers got their story.

A WINTER TALE

What former Dartmoor Prison Governor Basil Thomson called 'a sensational escape' occurred on 2nd January 1898. It involved convict William Morgan who had previously escaped from Parkhurst on the Isle of Wight before being transferred to Dartmoor. Perhaps because of this he was allocated a cell in one of the recently constructed 'modern' blocks which were considered to be escape proof. In those days only the ground floor cells had bars fitted to the windows, but they all had cast iron frames with panes a mere four inches square and a restricted opening far too small for a person to get through. However, Morgan was a desperate character with ten years penal servitude ahead of him and on the day of his escape, either through negligence by or with the connivance of a warder, had smuggled the head of a sledgehammer into the prison on his return from labour.

It was a Sunday evening and suppers had just been served when Morgan literally made his 'break' by smashing through the iron framework of his cell window with the hammer head. He timed the blows to coincide with a ritual sound he'd heard hundreds of times, the rhythmical banging of cell doors by the warders (hence the term 'banged up'). The aperture he made in the limited time available to him was surprisingly small, prompting the comment that it was not the first time an escapee had demonstrated an opening large enough for the head to pass through was large enough for the body too (in 1851 a prisoner called Thomas Clutch actually slipped between the bars to freedom). Morgan had to strip in order to squeeze through the jagged opening and injured himself in the process. After throwing his clothes out he lowered himself to the ground using an improvised rope made from twisted bed sheets and climbed over the prison wall with the aid of a discarded wooden pole he found in the yard.

He afterwards admitted he had singled out a particular house he could see from his cell window on the Rundlestone — Two Bridges road which he intended breaking into for a change of clothes — every escaped convict's need. However, to his dismay the place was still lit and there was the barking of dogs on his approach, leaving him to face the rigours of the open moor in the blackness of night and the winter cold. He kept going for two nights and a day without food or drink, and bleeding from the wounds he sustained climbing out of his damaged cell window. On Tuesday he was on the upper reaches of the River Teign, close to Scorhill stone circle. He was surveying a house which he contemplated raiding after dark in the hope of finding food when he was seen by a farmer named Perryman who, observing he had no hat or coat, guessed at once who he was. Morgan made a run for it but the farmer urged his dog after him and it clamped its jaws into Morgan's breeches, slowing him sufficiently for the farmer to catch up. The convict faced

Mr. Perryman's levelled shotgun defiantly, believing it to be empty until he was shown the cartridge in the breech. That settled it. The fugitive went before his captor to the very house he had been planning to break into that night, instead of which he was the 'guest' of kindly Mr. Perryman who gave him bread and cheese and some milk before taking him to Chagford where the local Constable took charge of him.

William Morgan displayed exceptional fortitude in his unsuccessful escape bid, and he taught the prison authorities a lesson because every cell window was later fitted with bars.

Escaped convict avoiding detection. (From an old print, reproduced courtesy of Prison Officer Mike Chamberlain).

BRIEF ENCOUNTERS

The countless escape stories relating to Dartmoor Prison have a special interest and excitement all their own. To this day and with the prison downgraded to Category 'C' an escape still makes headlines in the local press. Yet the hardships endured and the courage of those who pursue them are often ignored as are the several less dramatic occurrences involving the public.

Schoolmaster Terry Hopkins of Totnes relates the following story: "I was only a lad in 1963 and went one day for a cycle ride near Bow in mid-Devon when I was approached by a disreputable looking man, unshaven and wearing a blue denim jacket. 'Hello mate,' he said 'where's the nearest telephone?' I took him to a country house close by where I knew the occupants had a phone and left him at the entrance not giving the matter another thought. The next day I was taken aback to read in the local paper an escaped prisoner from Dartmoor Prison had telephoned from a house near Bow to give himself up – he'd had enough of sleeping rough and going hungry. You never know who you are talking to, do you?"

In that same year a young lady living in the South Hams bought a local paper on her way home from work. A headline about a prisoner on the run from Dartmoor Prison caught her eye with a photograph beneath. Imagine her surprise and horror to see her cousin's face staring at her. Her father was very strict and had taken great pains to keep the matter secret both within the family and without which is why she had no knowledge of her cousin's misdemeanours or imprisonment. His name was Crook.

Sometimes people have a premonition or a strong instinct (Americans call it a 'hunch') that all is not as it should be. The late Mr. Ron Chudley of Exmouth, a former *Western Morning News* reporter told the author about an incident from his young days when an escaped convict story always made good copy. He was sent to Dartmoor to report on a breakout. On his way he passed through Merrivale and was suddenly overcome by an irresistible conviction the fugitive must be hiding in the quarry there. So very strong was this feeling he spent a long time standing in the gateway looking for any sign of movement but finally decided to go on to the prison and await developments. He was there with several others when the recaptured man was brought in. The prisoner spotted Ron and yelled 'I know you!' Everybody stared. 'You're the bloke wot was looking straight at me in the quarry'. Ron's intuition was right after all.

It was no joke for a man who absconded when Basil Thomson was Governor (1903 – 1907). In his book *The Criminal* Mr. Thomson describes how this man got away in atrocious weather when he himself joined the hunt for him on horseback. He was the one who found him shivering and irresolute, anxious only to be recaptured. 'In fact when he saw me', wrote the Governor 'instead of running away he approached me and scrambled over a wall to my side. I have never seen so miserable an object'. Dartmoor itself can be a harsh prison.

Prison Officer Mike Chamberlain recalls an incident when an inmate was recaptured just in time to save his life. It happened several years ago in the vicinity of Long Plantation where a work party had stopped for lunch. It was a freezing February day, crisp and clear, and the prison officer in charge was snug and warm huddled close to a cast iron 'pot bellied stove' sharing hot soup with the ten inmates he was responsible for. *Or were they ten in number?* A blast of cold air turned his attention to the open door of their hut where stood a Principal Officer, a rare visitor to that location on such a day. 'Everything O.K.?' he asked. 'Yes thanks' was the casual reply. 'Just thought I'd ask because driving by I noticed a man running across a field towards Beardown'. 'Well all mine are here — all ten of them' and the officer made a quick check, but to his horror only nine inmates were present. 'Where's Foxie?' he asked. 'In the toilet Guv' someone said. There were two portaloos and both were unoccupied. Stark realisation and a radio message 'There's one away' preceded a prompt return to the prison and a search for the missing man. The police dogs found Foxie who took refuge up a tree with a helicopter hovering overhead. He had no chance and surrendered. Apparently he had worn his gym vest and shorts underneath his work clothes and after discarding his outer garments made a dash hoping to be mistaken for a 'jogger' (in sub-zero temperatures and wearing steel toe-capped boots). When he was returned to the prison the hospital staff checked him out, diagnosed hypothermia and put him at once into a hot bath and gave him hot tea. He was on the television news that night but could just as easily been in a coffin after risking certain death on the moor lightly clad in the bitter cold.

For Police Constable Simon Dell, M.B.E; Q.C.B. such considerate attention was not forthcoming. Apart from the risk of physical attack from suspects resisting arrest, public sympathy often sides with the villain whilst our hard-pressed policemen regularly have to 'grin and bear it' (it is frequently the case today). In P.C. Dell's own words:

'A prison escapee still represents a serious risk to those pursuing him and I have on a few occasions been on the receiving end of a few well-aimed blows from some of them. Some years ago during a bad winter I recaptured an escaping convict from the marshes at the head of the River Walkham to where I had chased him. He was in a hypothermic state after we had both got quite a soaking. I took him to Tavistock Hospital for care and attention where my captive was received with warmth and sympathy and remarks of "You poor man," and "What have they done to you", whilst I had to sit outside in the cold. Such is life I thought and such is 'justice' — long may it continue'.

JOE DENNY - THE MAN WHO BROKE
INTO DARTMOOR PRISON

The story of how a black man, who was released from Dartmoor after serving an eight year sentence, returned the following year with the specific intention of breaking *into* the prison is without precedent and tinged with sadness. His motive was revenge for the alleged ill-treatment he had endured. During his subsequent trial the prosecution produced 124 prison reports against him for breaches of discipline, for which he was punished by flogging, solitary confinement and periods on restricted diet. Was he persecuted because of his colour, as he claimed, or was he the troublesome nuisance the prison officials made him out to be? Many an officer today will tell you there are men in their charge who are sick in mind and should not be in prison at all. Whatever the truth may be, when a hardened criminal weeps in the dock, possibly with frustration at not being able to convince the court what he says is true, the reader may conclude there was cause to question a regime that broke men's hearts and led to several warders resigning year by year.

Prison conditions were harsh in the 19th century and the regulations laid down by the State applied to every prison, but Dartmoor's unique location high on a windswept moor, isolated it from the outside world. Consequently the regime was at the whim of those in charge. Outside work ceased only when there was heavy rain or snow, or because a Dartmoor mist restricted visibility and thus the degree of security; in addition, some discontented warders deliberately gave the convicts a hard time. It is against this background we should judge an episode which can only be described as bizarre. Joseph Denny had served time in three prisons:

Six months at Carmarthen Prison for housebreaking.

Seven years in Liverpool Jail for manslaughter.

Eight years at Dartmoor for felony.

After his release from Dartmoor Prison on 8th January 1889 he spent nine months at sea, voyaging to the West Indies among other places. When he got back to England he set out on foot from London and made his way to Princetown seeking revenge for the alleged injustices he'd suffered at Dartmoor. In the summer of 1890 he was seen in the streets of Tavistock with a group of performing dogs and monkeys; he also turned up at Princetown where he presented his animal show on some waste ground the day before his escapade.

Just before midnight on Saturday 16th August the Prison Governor, Capt. Oswald William Every, was making his final visit of the day to ensure all was well. Suddenly the alarm bells rang. The bells were activated by wires strung along the inside of the perimeter wall and were designed to detect anyone trying to escape. A search party was organised and Joe Denny was discovered hiding in the W.C. adjacent to the carpenter's shop. He was recognised immediately by a surprised warder who exclaimed 'Hello Joe, it's you is it?' When Denny could offer no explanation for being there he was handcuffed and handed over to the local policeman who lived in Princetown and had a 'lock up' in his house.

When the Prison Chaplain called next day (Sunday) the constable was unwilling at first to open the cell door because of Denny's threatening manner. Denny had told him he had come to set fire to the prison and murder 'Flash Hardy', the Chief Warder, 'and murder him I will!' he declared. The Chaplain, Reverend Clifford Rickards, B.A., an experienced and kindly man, managed to calm the prisoner and give him some sound advice. He describes the interview and subsequent events in his book *A Prison Chaplain on Dartmoor* (E. Arnold, London, 1920) in a way that suggests he had a genuine sympathy for the fellow. Perhaps he knew about the alleged cruelty meted out to him in prison, over which of course he had no control.

Earlier that morning a prison farm worker found a dead sheep hidden in a cow shed; it had been bludgeoned to death and a large piece, cut from a shoulder, appeared to have been eaten raw. Denny admitted to this, saying: 'I have done fifteen years for the old woman and she ought to be able to stand a sheep or two' (presumably the term 'old woman' referred to Queen Victoria). He was taken to Tavistock on Sunday afternoon and charged with prison breaking before Magistrate Mr. W.S. Rosevere, who remanded him in custody until Tuesday 19th August. It is interesting to note Denny was taken back to Princetown to be locked up because the River Tavy had recently burst its banks and the police cells, which were (and still are) below river level, had been flooded.

When he appeared before Mr. Rosevere again the charges were:

1. Breaking into Dartmoor Prison for an unlawful purpose.
2. Being on prison premises for the purpose of setting fire to the building.
3. Killing and stealing a sheep, property of the prison authorities.

The newspapers described Denny as being a native of Barbados, about forty four years old, 'with a higher forehead than is usual for a Negro and intelligent features'. He was above average intelligence and wore spectacles which, in repose, gave him 'a benign look'. The courtroom was packed with spectators.

Evidence was given by the Governor, Capt. Every, Warder John Stacey (who had apprehended Denny) and Chief Warder Augustus Hardy, who produced a length of rope which, he said, must have been used by the defendant for the break in. It was a length of clothes line, one end of which had been attached to a post in the Deputy Governor's garden (his residence was adjacent to the boundary wall and to the left of the main prison entrance); the other end was hanging over the wall on the inside, presumably to enable the intruder to get back out. During the hearing the defendant was allowed to question witnesses, but had little to ask that was significant except when Mr. Hardy showed the court the rope. Prisoner: 'What was the length of rope hanging over the wall?' Hardy: 'I should think about six foot'. Prisoner: 'A good drop for you!' (referring to a hanging). There was uproar and laughing from onlookers and order was restored only by Mr. Rosevere threatening to clear the court. Denny was unable to contain his obvious resentment and shedding his 'benign appearance' rendered a sweeping condemnation of Dartmoor Prison. He described being put in irons and being confined to a dark cell because he was 'a coloured man and plain spoken'. The Chief Warder, he said, had put him through the most cruel punishments, being 'deputy governor, clergyman, doctor, and everything else'. In all the prisons he'd been in there was no officer given so much power as the Chief Warder at Dartmoor who had treated him

Captain Oswald Every, Dartmoor Prison Governor 1880-1890. (Courtesy of Dartmoor Prison Heritage Centre).

worse than a dog. Despite warnings by the Magistrate 'not to be foolish' and 'not to say any more', the defendant declared he could not get that man out of his mind. 'If he were released now', he went on, 'I could not leave until I put him in his grave'. His idea had been to set fire to the prison, giving prisoners 'a chance to escape from hell', and lie in wait for the Chief Warder, who would be the first to be called in case of fire, when he would have used the knife on him (he was relieved of a box of matches and a knife when he was arrested).

Throughout this tirade the prisoner glared at Mr. Hardy and repeated he 'would mount the gallows with a contented heart tomorrow' if he could send that rogue (pointing to the Chief Warder) before him. Denny was committed to the forthcoming Devon Assizes under the Larceny Act, having condemned himself. He was held at Exeter Prison until 2nd December when he was brought before Judge Sir William Grantham. In the interim period the following letter was published in the *Exeter Flying Post* dated 30th August:

'I wish to write a few lines about ex-convict Denny who is now awaiting trial for breaking in to Dartmoor Prison. What he says in his statement is perfectly true.

I was at Dartmoor with him for more than two years, and during the greater part of that time he was under punishment; but for his iron constitution he would never have come out alive. He was several times flogged and continually under bread and water. He was for several months wearing the black dress and fourteen pounds of iron chains and in the winter of 1888 he was sent out to work on the bogs with a cold canvas dress on – he was treated worse than a dog'.*

The contents of this letter did not reach Denny and no mention of it was made at his trial. The prosecutor at the Assizes, after saying it was one of the most extraordinary cases he had ever encountered, proceeded to call witnesses who repeated the evidence they had given to the Tavistock magistrate. Chief Warder Hardy was interrupted several times by the defendant who complained about how cruelly he'd been treated by him. Mr. Hardy replied he had nothing to do with punishments or the withholding of privileges; his duty was to see reports were logged and he did not attend adjudications. When the defendant recalled being handcuffed and left in the cold whilst with a work party on the moor, Mr. Hardy said 'If men refused to work they were handcuffed but were free to walk about'. Captain Every, the Prison Governor, confirmed he had known the prisoner for a number of years, having had him in his custody, but denied saying 'I expected as much' when Denny was apprehended. 'We don't expect to find people trying to get inside', he remarked, 'they generally try to get out!' (laughter in court). The Exeter Prison doctor testified how he had answered a complaint by Denny about being ill; in fact he had refused to eat and had to be removed to a special cell with a warder in attendance to ensure he ate and would be fit to appear in court. When the night watchman at Exeter said Denny had confessed to breaking into Dartmoor to get his revenge on the Chief Warder, Denny, in a desperate attempt to refute him said he'd often been told he talked in his sleep.

It was all downhill for the prisoner now and when he addressed the jury he broke down and wept, acknowledging he had malice towards Mr. Hardy and had sought revenge, but he was then 'in a passion' and asked for mercy, being a coloured man far from his native land. Judge Grantham was unmoved. Dartmoor Prison's Governor had acted with great discretion, kindness and consideration for him he said. Chief Warder Hardy could not give effect to any ill feeling he might have had, declared the Judge and he did not see he had any ill feeling. He sentenced Denny to twelve months hard labour. Joe Denny died in prison. For all his misdeeds, he may have been harbouring a genuine grievance and died a broken man; maybe the physical effects of the punishments he'd received accelerated his demise; perhaps he was mentally unbalanced. Whatever the truth of the matter, his story is a frightening indictment of the penal system in Victorian England and goes a long way towards explaining why a man broke **into** Dartmoor Prison after getting **out.**

*'Black dress'- yellow and black uniform worn by convicts who either assaulted a warder or attempted to escape. The fourteen pounds of leg irons or chains were a practical deterrent.

'Canvas dress' - worn by convicts who, as a means of protest, tore up their clothes.

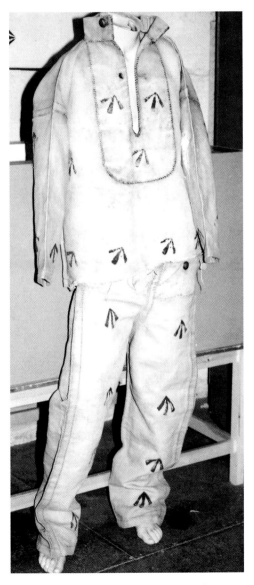

Canvas uniform worn by men who for whatever reason, tore up their clothing. (Courtesy of Dartmoor Prison Heritage Centre).